Inner Revolution

Embracing Change to Achieve Greatness

By: Michael Stevenson, Alnita Coulter, David King,
Marcia Souza, Jennifer Altimore, Mystral Echavarria,
Dawn Aldredge, Rachel Bock, Becky Parker,
Dr. Sharon Ostermeir, Isabella Godinez, Shreve Gould,
Jo Ann Long, Rev. Donna Baranyay, Troy and Nadirah Lugg,
Michael Roth, Carolyn Cahn, Brandy Lovingier,
Fernanda Diaz, Joanne Klepal, Sam Wakefield

Edited by: Elizabeth Garvey

Inner Revolution

Copyright © 2024 Authority Alliance Publishing

ISBN: 978-1-946607-30-0

Published by Authority Alliance Publishing in the USA

All Rights Reserved. No part of this text may be reproduced, stored in a retrieval system, or transmitted by any means, electronic, mechanical, photocopying, desktop publishing, recording, or otherwise, without permission from the publisher. No patent liability is assumed with respect to the use of the information contained herein. While every precaution has been taken in the preparation of this book, the publisher and author assume no responsibility for errors or omissions. Neither is any liability assumed for damages resulting from the use of the information contained herein.

All terms mentioned in this book that are known to be trademarks, registered trademarks, or service marks have been appropriately capitalized and are denoted with a ®, a ™ or an ℠. The publisher cannot attest to the accuracy of this information. Use of a term in this book should not be regarded as affecting the validity of any registered trademark, trademark, or service mark.

The opinions expressed in each individual chapter are the viewpoints of each individual author, and do not necessarily reflect the viewpoints, values, or opinions of Transform Destiny, its agents and employees, or any other author in the book.

Table of Contents

Introduction 1
Michael Stevenson 3
Alnita Coulter 17
David King 29
Marcia Souza 41
Jennifer Altimore 55
Mystral Echavarria 65
Dawn Aldredge 77
Rachel Bock 91
Becky Parker 103
Sharon Ostermeir 115
Isabella Godinez 127
Shreve Gould 139
Jo Ann Long 153
Rev. Donna Baranyay 165
Nadirah & Troy Lugg 177
Michael Roth 189
Carolyn Cahn 201
Brandy Lovingier 213
Fernanda Diaz 225
Joanne Klepal 237
Sam Wakefield 249

Introduction

Nearly every person in the world wants more out of their life. Why? Because they don't have the things they want: more money, more love, more health, more things.

As a coach for nearly 25 years, I have discovered that this comes down to a difference between "wanting" and "willing."

For example, most people want more money, but they're not willing to get more money. Anybody can get more money. Literally, anybody. I don't care what situation you're in, there are an unlimited number of ways to get money.

You could take another job. You could start a craft and sell it on Etsy. You could get certified in Neuro-Linguistic Programming and help people, as most of the authors of this book have done. And a million other ideas.

So, why don't people do it? The Comfort Zone.

In this book, 21 experts on mindset and motivation using tools like Neuro-Linguistic Programming, TIME Techniques, Hypnotherapy, and Coaching, will help you learn how to get out of your comfort zone and embrace change to achieve greatness. We hope this book has a profound impact on your life and that you have a profound impact on the lives of others.

Michael Stevenson, November, 2024
Authority Alliance Publishing

Inner Revolution: Embracing Change to Achieve Greatness

Inner Revolution: Embracing Change to Achieve Greatness

Resilience: The Key to Achievement

Michael Stevenson, Master Trainer of NLP, Mindset Expert

Resilience is the stuff that heroes are made of, but it's not something we're born with.

It's built, molded, and refined through experiences—often challenging and heartbreaking ones. Adversity, as painful as it may be, is one of the most powerful forces that shape who we become.

It teaches us to rise from the ashes, to bounce back, and to grow stronger.

But what if someone hasn't faced great adversity? Does that mean they are doomed to live without resilience?

Absolutely not.

Resilience is something you can borrow, lean on, and develop even if your path hasn't been filled with the obstacles others have endured.

The certainty that things will turn out okay, no matter the difficulty, can be shared by those who have walked through fire. The beauty of resilience is that it's transferable; it's something we can pass on.

In my life, adversity was the crucible that forged my fearlessness. I was *forced* out of my comfort zone for the first half of my life.

From being born to a teenage mother with Borderline Personality Disorder to growing up in poverty to losing everything—twice—I've learned that it's not about avoiding hardship, but about embracing the lessons that come from it, trusting in your ability to rise above, and taking bold risks; knowing that, no matter what happens, you will be okay.

Born Into Adversity

My life started under difficult circumstances. My mother was only fourteen when I was born. She was still a child, forced to take on the responsibilities of adulthood far too early.

We had little. We lived in abject poverty. For as long as I can remember, my early years were shaped by scarcity, uncertainty, a deep sense of struggle, and visits from Child Protective Services.

But this struggle was my "normal." I knew nothing else. And in that environment, I learned an invaluable lesson: resilience is not about avoiding difficulty—it's about thriving within it.

When you grow up with nothing, every day becomes a lesson in survival. I saw my mother and stepfather try to make the most of what we had, and even in the toughest times, there was always a sense of hope. I realize now that hope was resilience. It was the belief that no matter how difficult things were, they would somehow get better.

But that wasn't the end of my struggles. When I was nine, we faced a disaster that would forever change my life.

From Having Nothing to Losing Everything

Inner Revolution: Embracing Change to Achieve Greatness

While we had little, in December 1982, a massive, historical flood wiped out everything my family owned.

We lived in Times Beach, Missouri, a small town seized by the Environmental Protection Agency and destroyed because of toxic dioxin contamination after the flood. All I knew was our home—a tiny, single-wide mobile home in a tiny trailer park—was destroyed. What little we had built over the years was gone. We had nothing.

The weight of that loss was far too heavy for a child to carry. The flood didn't just wash away our possessions; it washed away the sense of security we had clung to.

We were forced to move to California to live with my grandparents. That trauma had lasting ramifications, from me wetting the bed again at nine years old and having intense nightmares to failing at school and feeling like an outcast among the California kids who had a vastly different culture than I was used to.

But what I didn't realize at the time was that this moment, this catastrophic loss would become a cornerstone of my resilience.

When you lose everything, you realize how little "everything" really is. Material possessions, as important as they seem, are fleeting. What truly matters is your ability to pick yourself up, to start over, and to rebuild. The flood taught me that loss is not the end—it's an opportunity for a new beginning.

And when you start again with nothing, you carry with you the most important thing: the knowledge that you can survive anything.

"When you ain't got nothing, you got nothing to lose."—Bob Dylan

Just ten years later, at 19, I found myself homeless. After a series of unfortunate events, I lost everything once more.

For six months, I had no place to call home. It was one of the darkest periods of my life. Homelessness strips away your identity. You feel invisible, isolated, and completely untethered from the world around you.

Homelessness taught me that resilience isn't just about enduring hardship—it's about trusting that <u>every</u> setback is temporary.

Life moves in cycles. There are highs and lows, but nothing lasts forever. That certainty allowed me to keep going, even when things felt impossible. It's the same certainty that I now pass on to others who face their challenges.

Building Success Through Risk and Fearlessness

Looking back, I realize that these early experiences—being born into poverty, losing everything in the flood, and becoming homeless—were gifts. They gave me something far more valuable than material success. They gave me fearlessness.

I have learned to be grateful for my challenges.

When you have nothing to lose, you're free to take risks. And when you've survived the worst, you know that failure isn't fatal. It's just another part of the process. I carried that mindset into my professional life, and it's the driving force behind my success.

In 2000, I founded *Transform Destiny*, a company dedicated to transforming people's lives through Neuro-Linguistic Programming (NLP), hypnosis, coaching, and personal development.

The company started small, but I wasn't afraid to dream big. I took risks that others might have shied away from. And those risks paid off. Over the years, *Transform Destiny* grew into one of the top NLP training institutes in the world.

But it wasn't just about the business. The resilience I had built over the years allowed me to push boundaries in my personal life, too.

Homeless Again at 42 Years Old

When we got together in 2012, as our relationship was becoming serious, Kayla and I started talking about life's goals. Where would we live? Kids or no kids? When would we retire?

We both agreed that we wanted to travel. A LOT. We initially talked about having a trip somewhere once every six weeks. But we wanted more.

I was inspired by my grandparents' dream to travel to the US. My grandmother would always get a starry look in her eyes when she would talk about it. She told me, "Someday, when your grandpa retires, we're going to sell everything, buy an RV, and travel full-time all around the US."

They never got to achieve that dream.

My grandmother was diagnosed with advanced lung disease at 52 and prescribed an oxygen tank. By 54, she was on full-time oxygen. By 55, she was bedridden. And at 58, she passed away.

Besides how devastated I was at the loss of my "Gramma," I was heartbroken to know that the dream they had their entire life was never realized.

All those wasted years of working hard to "earn" the right to enjoy life, what we call retirement, thrown down the drain.

So, on Valentine's Day 2015, Kayla and I made a **bold** decision.

We sold almost everything we owned—our worldly possessions—except what we could fit into four suitcases, two laptop bags, and two backpacks and bought a one-way ticket to London. Where would we go after that with no home to return to? Only time will tell.

We wanted to be free to travel, to explore, and to live life on our terms. It was a tremendous risk—at least according to everyone who we told about this adventure.

People were aghast. Some people were mortified.

"Where will you live?" people questioned. "In hotels," we would assure them.

"But how will you eat?" they would ask, wide-eyed. "In restaurants," we would answer.

"What if you have an accident in another country?" they'd worry. "They have hospitals wherever we'll be," we would say.

People told us we'd be unhappy without a community, a church, routines, and the other things that people find so comforting in their lives.

In almost every interaction, they would have these questions. People just couldn't wrap their heads around what we were doing.

With every question we would answer, we were easing *their* fears.

But we weren't afraid. We had both been out of our comfort zones many times before.

I learned that as long as you have each other and the belief that things will turn out okay, you need little else.

That decision—to let go of material possessions and embrace a life of freedom—was one of the best I've ever made. It was a reminder that resilience isn't just about bouncing back from hardship; it's about letting go of fear, trusting in your ability to adapt, and taking bold action when the opportunity arises.

We traveled full-time, visiting 55 countries and over 120 cities, and we lived more life in those five years than 100 people could live in their entire lifetimes.

Borrowing Resilience

Now, you might read this and think, "That's great for you, Michael, but I haven't faced those kinds of challenges." And that's okay.

Resilience isn't reserved for those who have lived through great adversity. It can be borrowed and learned.

If you haven't faced significant hardship, you can still cultivate resilience by learning from the experiences of others. Surround yourself with people who have walked through fire and come out stronger.

Listen to their stories, absorb their lessons, and let their certainty become yours. When you see others have survived and thrived, you believe you can, too.

Resilience is also built by embracing small challenges. You don't need a catastrophic event to develop strength. Every time you face a setback, no matter how small, you practice resilience.

Each challenge, each obstacle, is a chance to grow, to learn, and to strengthen your resolve. But you have to learn to embrace challenges, not avoid them.

The Power of Risk

Inner Revolution: Embracing Change to Achieve Greatness

One of the most important lessons I've learned is that resilience and risk go hand in hand. When you're resilient, you're not afraid to take risks. And when you take risks, you open yourself up to new possibilities, new rewards, and new levels of success.

If I had let fear hold me back, I would never have achieved what I have today. *Transform Destiny* wouldn't exist. *Ethical Marketing Academy* wouldn't exist. And I wouldn't have had the freedom to live the life I dreamed of with Kayla.

Fear is the enemy of progress. It keeps you stuck, paralyzed, and afraid to act. But when you've built resilience, fear loses its power. You know no matter what happens, you can handle it. You've been through worse, and you've come out stronger.

In every great story ever told—from ancient tales of lore, such as *The Iliad* and *The Odyssey*, to modern epics like *The Lord of the Rings* and *Star Wars*—the main character always goes through a "hero's journey." It's the required ingredient.

On a hero's journey, our beloved character starts in a place of peace, joy, and wholeness. Life is grand. Then, there comes a "call to adventure." Frodo must leave the Shire. Luke is called to save Princess Leia. They must leave the safety of what is known and venture into the unknown.

They must exit their *comfort zone*.

After challenges, trials, and tribulations, they overcome their challenges (and the challenges are always internal, even though there's an external "enemy"), and finally come back to a place of peace, joy, and wholeness.

While the hero's journey is always depicted as a circle, it isn't. It's an upward spiral. Because our hero does not come back the same; they have leveled up.

All the great stories we know include the main character leaving their comfort zone for an adventure... when was the last time *you* had an adventure?

Embracing Your Resilience

Whether you've faced adversity, resilience is within your reach, because it's a choice. It's a mindset, a way of seeing the world, and a belief in your ability to overcome whatever challenges come your way.

It's the certainty that, no matter how difficult things get, you will be okay.

Remember, resilience is not just about bouncing back—it's about bouncing forward. It's about using every setback as a springboard for growth, every failure as a lesson, and every challenge as an opportunity to become stronger, wiser, and more fearless.

You don't have to wait for a flood, homelessness, a wizard, a Dark Lord of the Sith, or some other life-altering event to build your resilience. You can start now by embracing challenges, taking risks, and trusting in your ability to adapt and thrive.

Inner Revolution: Embracing Change to Achieve Greatness

So, this is it... your *call to adventure*. Your greatness awaits.

"Twenty years from now, you will be more disappointed by the things that you didn't do than by the ones you did. So, throw off the bowlines. Sail away from the safe harbor. Catch the trade winds in your sails. Explore. Dream. Discover."—Mark Twain (1835-1910)

About Michael Stevenson

Michael Stevenson is the Founder and CEO of Transform Destiny and a Master Trainer of Neuro-Linguistic Programming (NLP). With over 25 years of experience, he has helped countless coaches, therapists, and business owners take their lives and businesses to the next level.

Michael is a best-selling author of multiple books and co-starred in the documentary The Evolution of Success. He has a passion for helping people become the best versions of themselves and to live their dreams. He often uses NLP techniques to help his clients reach their goals.

Michael is an expert at helping people understand how to use their minds and language to create positive change in their lives. His unique approach to personal and professional development has earned him the respect of his peers and clients alike. He is a highly sought-after speaker at conferences and workshops around the world.

Michael is committed to helping people achieve success and reach their dreams. His passion is helping them learn how to use their minds to create the life they desire. He believes anyone can reach their goals with the right tools and attitude. He is committed to helping others reach their dreams and live the life they've always wanted.

Michael's gift: www.InnerRevolutionBook.com/gift/MichaelS

Remember, resilience is not just about bouncing back—it's about bouncing forward.

Inner Revolution: Embracing Change to Achieve Greatness

Inner Revolution: Embracing Change to Achieve Greatness

Breakthrough To Your B.R.I.L.L.I.A.N.C.E.

Alnita Coulter, MNLP, MTT, MHt, MSC, and Trainer of NLP

You are brilliant!

According to the Dunning-Kruger effect, most people think they are more intelligent than they actually are. Yet, you may still not see yourself as brilliant because you hold brilliance to a higher standard.

If you believe that the average person feels more intellectually competent than they truly are, then why do you and others often remark that something feels missing or that you're underperforming in your lives during private conversations?

If the thought of someone using the term "brilliant" to describe you makes you feel uneasy or like there's been a colossal blunder, you are not alone.

Just as each individual has unique fingerprints, your level of brilliance—or what makes you feel brilliant—differs from anyone else's. Whether you acknowledge this to others or keep it to yourself, you know when you are not living up to your potential.

An uncut diamond lacks the brilliance of its cut and polished counterpart. Without the carefully crafted facets that bring out the stone's beauty, an uncut diamond can easily be overlooked and undervalued. However, the skillful cuts made by a gem cutter help to showcase the diamond's natural beauty, and sometimes those cuts even use the diamond's flaws to enhance its overall appearance.

Just as a lapidarist transforms an uncut diamond into a brilliant masterpiece, it is essential for you to become your own gem cutter so that you can uncover the most brilliant version of yourself.

So, if brilliance is excellence or distinction in physical or mental ability; exceptional talent, then what exactly is breaking through to your brilliance? It is about becoming the person who you have always wanted or hoped to be.

You come into this world with a name you didn't choose and, some believe, a family you didn't select. You spend a lifetime trying to grow into the expectations placed upon you. While some easily fit into the mold, others yearn for something more. Whether it's living your purpose or simply a temporary position along your path, you deserve the right to shine.

Unfortunately, discovering what makes you happy or fulfilled can sometimes feel elusive. **Breakthrough to Your Brilliance** is a two-part system designed to help you figure out how to shine in all areas of your life.

There are two five-step parts to the **Breakthrough to Your Brilliance** system.

Break is the first part of the system. It involves five steps that focus on breaking down the pieces needed to uncover your brilliance. Through is the second part of the system, comprised of five steps that focus on the actions you need to perform to embody and live your brilliance.

Both parts of the system combine to create a roadmap that shows you how to become the person you want to be as you **Breakthrough to Your Brilliance**.

Part 1:
Break comprises: **B**reakthrough, **R**eflection, **I**nspiration, **L**ove , **L**everage

1. Breakthrough. Before you can figure out who you want to be, it's also important to figure out who you don't want to be. Have a stack of sticky notes handy so you can write your ideas. Make a list. It will help you set parameters. Next, create a list of characteristics that reflect who you want to be.

Centering yourself will make this easier. Close your eyes and take three deep breaths. Each time, breathe in for four seconds, hold for four seconds, and breathe out for four seconds.

Then go into a heightened-focused or **Shine State**, which will allow you to bypass your conscious mind and tap into the power of your subconscious mind. Getting into **Shine State** will help you more easily discover what will allow you to truly live your brilliance, what you are trying to accomplish, and who you are trying to become.

To get into **Shine State**, sit with your shoulders relaxed and your head leveled. Without moving your head, lift your eyes to a 45-degree angle and focus on a single spot on the wall.

You should not feel any strain while doing this. As your eyes rest on the spot, hold your hands next to your face and just out of the edge of your vision and allow your vision to expand outward. You should be able to see your fingers wiggle out of the corner of your eye. You will notice the awareness of your surroundings will grow. Once you feel this happen, gently lower your eyes while continuing to keep your focus outward.

You can check to see if you are in **Shine State** by wiggling your fingers right out of your peripheral view. If you can no longer see them, simply raise your eyes up to a 45-degree angle again and allow your vision to expand. You can use this focused state any time you need to tap into your subconscious mind, like studying.

Once you are in **Shine State**, ask yourself the question, "What are the things I would be great at doing that would bring me the biggest satisfaction?" Don't censor them. Write one idea per sticky note. Keep writing until you run out of ideas. Once you have the sticky notes, arrange them first in an order of what will give you the most satisfaction to the one that will give you the least satisfaction.

Make a note of this or take a photo. Make sure you can read the notes in the photo. Rearrange the sticky notes in order from the one that will be easiest for you to accomplish to the one that will be the most difficult for you to accomplish. Take a photo or make a note of this and compare the lists.

Do you notice any similarities in the list? Are there things on the list you would like to eliminate simply because of feasibility, available resources, or the lack of joy that you think it will bring? It is important to note that some things on this list may not be what you genuinely want to do. There are things that may be on this list simply because you have been conditioned to do them.

If you have always included those items on your list because you felt you did not have permission to remove them, this is your lucky day. I give you full permission to eliminate them. In fact, allow yourself to exhale as you draw a big, thick line through those items. Part of the beauty of living your brilliance is that you do not have to "should" all over yourself, as in you should do this or you should do that. From henceforth and evermore, I release you from that. Note any feelings you might have as you embrace this new freedom.

When I was in college, I was talking with a student from Africa. Unfortunately, I do not recall which country. I asked him how he ended up in Augusta, GA. He said that back home you take tests that identify your ideal career path. According to his test, he should have become an engineer. So, if he went to college, he would have to go for engineering. However, he had a desire to become a doctor. Instead of burdening himself with "should," he broke free and left everything he knew just so he could live his brilliance and pursue his dream of becoming a doctor.

Now, think of the version of you that would show your true brilliance. You get bonus points if you smile when you think of this version of yourself. What's missing from what you currently do? What steps would you need to take in order to become this brilliant version of yourself? Take note. These are the things that will allow you to break through to what's keeping you from being your most brilliant self.

Once you figure out what you want to accomplish, get a picture of that in your mind and see yourself being, doing, and having it.

2. Reflection. Reflect on how each of these possibilities makes you feel. Try imagining what your life would be like if you were to do each of these things. How would your life be different? How would your life improve? Would these changes impact the lives of those around you? If so, how?

3. Inspiration. Create a vision board that contains pictures of the things you are trying to accomplish. You can do this digitally using **Canva** or other digital vision board apps such as **Perfectly Happy, Mind Movies,** or even **Pinterest**. You can also clip images from magazines. Find examples of people you admire that are doing the things you want to do.

Collect images of the goals you want to achieve and save them on your phone or computer. Create a dedicated album for these images. You can also arrange them on a piece of foam board or place them in the spaces where you envision achieving those goals. For instance, if you aspire to own a particular car, take a picture of yourself sitting in that car and keep it visible, such as attached to your visor or somewhere you can see it whenever you get into your current vehicle.

Use this method for both physical objects and intangible skills or achievements you wish to pursue.

4. Love. Of course, loving yourself is the starting point of breaking through to your brilliance. Loving the things that you decide to do or become is critical. Ask yourself, "If this was the only thing I could do for the rest of my life, would that be enough?" You may discover there are things you are good at that don't bring you joy. There also may be things you are not good at, that may be worth the extra effort it takes for you to learn how to do them. Breaking through to your brilliance is not just about doing the things at which you are good. It is about finding an intersection of things you are good at and also love.

5. Leverage. Whether it's time, resources, strengths, knowledge, or opportunities, make the most of what's available to you. Take an inventory so you know just what you are working with. Writing these things down might uncover ideas of which you did not readily think.

Now that you have identified who you want to become, it is crucial to identify the actions you must take to allow you to live your brilliance. The next steps focus on that.

Part 2.
Through comprises: **I**ntention, **A**bun**DANCE**, **N**ecessary, **C**ons istent **C**ommitment, **E**xcellence Infused with **E**nthusiasm

1. Intention. Setting clear, well-defined goals increases the likelihood of accomplishing them and allows you to stay on track. It is important to know where you are headed because as it was famously said in Alice and Wonderland, "If you don't know where you're going, any road will get you there." **Make sure you set clear deadlines and also schedule time to develop the items identified during the Break process.**

2. AbunDANCE. Have a daily motivational jam session with songs that hype you up and motivational messages that inspire you. Think of it as your Brilliance Soundtrack or personal theme song. While listening, see yourself successfully embodying all the brilliant things you want and seal it with a celebratory dance. Can't dance? It doesn't matter. It's about moving energy and creating a mind/body connection to your expanded brilliance, which will reinforce your actions. You can also listen to my AbunDANCE motivations at abundancemotivations.com.

3. Necessary. In trying to achieve anything, certain steps are required. Knowing what is crucial to ensure your success is important. When you create a plan, make sure you include these steps to guarantee that you will shine.

4. Consistent Commitment. Many think that consistency by itself is the secret to achieving anything. However, consistency is just the beginning. Committing and *then honoring* that commitment might be the most important step. Like Michael Stevenson says, when asked what the secret to his success is, he simply replies, "I honor my commitments." Make sure those commitments are brilliance-enhancing.

5. Excellence Infused with Enthusiasm. Once you figure everything out, then you have to operate with excellence. Make sure you cheer for yourself as loudly as you would cheer for someone else. Once you learn to greet your excellence with enthusiasm, you are well on your way to creating a brilliant new future!

Embrace Your Brilliance

Breaking through to your brilliance is a journey of self-discovery and transformation. Identify who you want to be, and the actions required to become that person. With the **Breakthrough to Your Brilliance** system, you have a roadmap that empowers you to navigate this journey. The two-part system—**Break** and **Through**—provides you with the tools to dismantle the barriers that hinder your growth and to take consistent, purposeful actions toward realizing your dreams.

You have the power to create a life where you shine effortlessly. By combining thoughtful decision-making with intentional actions, you will not only break through to your brilliance but also live a life of joy, fulfillment, and purpose. The journey begins now—embrace it, and let your brilliance illuminate the world around you!

About Alnita Coulter

Alnita Coulter, affectionately known as Amazing Alnita, is a Trainer and Master Practitioner of Neuro-Linguistic Programming (NLP), speaker, and author of both adult and children's books. She is passionate about helping individuals tap into their brilliance and transform their lives while healing their hurts and pursuing their dreams.

With a vibrant spirit, Amazing Alnita embraces life fully, dancing like no one's watching and inspiring others to do the same. She believes that personal transformation can be achieved through joy and fun. As a coach and consultant, she serves as a dedicated cheerleader for those on their journey to destiny, supporting them every step of the way.

She is a wanderer with the gift of wonder who delights in following her grandbabies around the world while sharing her experiences and insights. Check out her AbunDANCE motivational messages at AbunDanceMotivations.com. Connect with Amazing Alnita on Facebook at www.facebook.com/AmazingAlnita and explore more about her work at www.AmazingAlnita.com.

Get Amazing Alnita's gift:

www.InnerRevolutionBook.com/gift/Alnita

The journey begins now—embrace it, and let your brilliance illuminate the world around you!

Inner Revolution: Embracing Change to Achieve Greatness

Embrace the Fire for Change
David King, MNLP, MTT, MHt, MSC, EFT, FIT

Firewalking! Why on earth would you want to do that? In this chapter, you'll explore firewalking as more than a physical challenge. Firewalking symbolizes the inner strength required to face your fears, the courage to step into the unknown, and the willingness to embrace change. To walk on fire is to move beyond what seems impossible, to recognize that transformation comes from within.

You'll dive into the origins of fire walking, the psychology behind it, and the deep, symbolic connection between fire and personnel growth. The heat of the coals mirrors the intensity of your struggles, yet just like one can walk across the coals without being burned, you can navigate life's most challenging moments without being destroyed.

Firewalking Through Time and Cultures

Firewalking spans cultures, times, and geographies. From the Pacific islands to Greece, India, China, Australia, Africa, South America, and the United States, to name a few. It has been used in competition, sacrifices, healing ceremonies, to prove strength and courage, spiritual ceremonies, when accused of a crime if you walk without being burned you go free, team building, personnel growth, adrenaline rush, and pushes you out of your comfort zone, among others.

Here are some examples of how different cultures use firewalking. The Hirpi family in Ancient Rome firewalked as a sacrifice to Apollo. In Greece, there was a church fire in 1250, so the villagers' descendants walked through the flames every anniversary to honor the rescuers. Francis of Paola walked to help blacksmiths in Italy. In the Kalahari Desert, Bushman walked in healing ceremonies, and in Spain, people danced across the hot coals to celebrate the beginning of summer.

What about in North America? In the United States, there are four very popular uses: 1. Personal development, which includes helping to improve your health, increase your self-awareness, and create stronger bonds. 2. Overcoming limiting beliefs and prime concerns. 3. Inner transformation uses firewalking to shift limiting beliefs and thoughts to empowering beliefs. 4. Team building, businesses use firewalking to bring their team together and build a closer bond.

In Hawaii, it is said that while firewalking was not part of their culture, they would do a walk that was related. They would walk over barely crusted molten lava carrying tea leaves to protect them from Pele. Pele in the Hawaiian culture is the goddess of fire and volcanoes. It can also mean volcano, eruption, and lava flow.

Facing The Fire: Confronting Inner Fears

The actual fire you walk through is internal. When you face life's challenges, whether it be personal loss, career shifts, or major life changes, there is often uncertainty and doubt. Firewalking provides a physical manifestation of this internal struggle. Standing at the edge of a burning path, the heat and intensity mirror your inner turmoil.

But here is the lesson: It's not the fire that burns you, it's your mind. Fear is a powerful force, and it often convinces you that you are weaker than you are. To embrace fire is to challenge these limiting beliefs to recognize you are stronger than you can imagine. When you step on the coals, it is an act of defiance against mental barriers that are holding you back.

Fear is not to be taken lightly. It is part of being human, and it serves a purpose. When fear controls your choices, it stops you from growing. Firewalking teaches you that fear can be felt and acknowledged, however, it doesn't have to control you. You can take that step despite fear, and in doing so, you transform.

The Power of Belief and Transformation

Firewalking seems like a mystical or spiritual practice. This explains why people can walk across hot coals and not get burned. The coals are hot, sometimes reaching temperatures as high as 1200 degrees Fahrenheit, however, the act of walking quickly across minimizes the risk.

The key lies in that wood coals are poor conductors of heat. While extremely hot, they don't transfer heat to the skin as quickly as materials like metal would. The thickness and moisture of the skin on the soles of the feet act as a protective barrier, preventing immediate burns.

The scientific understanding underscores an important lesson: Many of the things you fear in life are like the coals. They may appear dangerous or unconquerable, but when approached with the right mindset and understanding, they are not as threatening as they seem. Firewalking reminds you that knowledge and perspective can turn fear into empowerment.

Stepping Into the Fire: Action Over Resistance

The hardest part of firewalking is often not the walk itself, but what leads to it. As you stand at the edge of the coals, your body responds to the perceived threat. Your heart races, your palms sweat, and every instinct tells you to turn back. This is the moment transformation begins, not in the walk, but in the decision to step forward.

To resist is natural. When you face something new or challenging, there is a voice inside that resists. It tells you to stay in your comfort zone, to avoid risk, to remain safe. However, by staying in that place, you get stuck. Growth requires discomfort; it requires you to step into the fire.

The moment you take that first step onto the coals, something shifts inside of you. You move from resistance to action, from fear to courage. Every step forward is a victory over the mental barriers that once held you back.

As you take each step on the coals, you may feel a surge of adrenaline, a heightened awareness of the heat beneath your feet. However, if you remain focused, keep moving, and trust, something magical happens. The fire does not burn. Instead, it becomes a pathway to empowerment.

The Journey of Transformation

Firewalking is a metaphor for the process of personal transformation. Just as each step across the coals brings you closer to the other side, every action you take toward your goals brings you closer to change. The fire does not vanish, but you learn to walk through it without being consumed.

This is the essence of embracing the fire, acknowledging that challenges and discomfort are part of the journey, but they do not have to stop you. You are stronger than you know.

Firewalking is as much the power of belief as it is about action. Those who walk across the coals do so because they believe they can. This belief is not blind faith, but a deep, inner knowing that they are capable of more than they realize.

In life, belief shapes your reality. The stories you tell yourself influence your decisions, your actions, and your outcomes. If you believe you can walk through the fire, whether literal or symbolic, you are more likely to succeed.

To embrace fire is to embrace a belief in yourself. It is recognizing that the limitations you perceive are often self-imposed and that you have the power to rewrite the narrative. Belief is the spark that ignites transformation.

Lessons From Firewalking

Firewalking offers profound lessons that extend beyond the experience itself. The ability to walk across burning coals without injury shows the mind's capacity to overcome fear and doubt. The act of walking through the fire reaches resilience, courage, and the power to act despite uncertainty.

In life, you will face fires and situations that challenge you, push you to your limits, and force you to confront your fears. But the lessons from the firewalking experience remind you that you are capable of more than you often give yourself credit for. You can face the heat, endure the discomfort, and come out the other side stronger.

Once you have walked through the fire, something shifts inside you. The experience of facing your fears and emerging unscathed changes the way you see yourself and the world. You realize that the limits you once accepted are no longer valid and that you are capable of far more than you imagined.

Firewalking leaves an impression. It serves as a reminder that challenges are not meant to stop you but to help you grow. Every time you face difficulty, you can embrace fire again.

In the end, firewalking is about change, about embracing the fire of transformation and emerging from it renewed. Change is inevitable, and fear and resistance often accompany it. But just like walking across the fire without being burned, you can navigate life's changes without being destroyed.

Embracing change means accepting that discomfort is part of the process, but it also means trusting in your ability to rise to the challenge. The fire will always be there, but so will your strength to walk through it.

By embracing the fire, you embrace change, and in doing so, you unlock the potential for growth, transformation, and a new way forward. It's the journey toward a stronger, more empowered self.

In conclusion, firewalking serves as a powerful metaphor for personal transformation and growth. It symbolizes the inner strength required to confront your fears, and the courage needed to step into the unknown. Through the act of walking across burning coals, you learn that fear, while ever-present, need not dictate your actions. Firewalking empowers you to rise above self-imposed limitations and embrace the potential for change and renewal.

Beyond its physical challenge, firewalking teaches you profound lessons about belief and resilience. The experience underscores that many perceived threats in life, much like coal, can be navigated successfully with the right mindset and understanding. By embracing the fire, you cultivate a belief in your capacity to overcome obstacles, transforming fear into a catalyst for action and empowerment.

Guiding the Flames of Change

Firewalking invites you to redefine the boundaries of what you believe is possible. It leaves an impression, reminding you that challenges are not there to halt your progress but to propel you forward. By choosing to walk through the fire, you embrace change, unlock your potential, and embark on a journey toward a stronger, more empowered self. The fire will always be present, but so too will your strength to walk through it unharmed.

The scientific explanation of firewalking further illuminates the lesson that many perceived threats in life, much like the hot coals, are not as difficult as they appear when approached with the right mindset and understanding. Firewalking teaches resilience and the strength to act despite fear. As you embrace the fire, you embrace change, unlocking the potential for growth and a new way forward. This journey of transformation echoes the broader journey of life, encouraging you to trust in your strength and ability to rise to any challenge.

So, I would like to leave you with a story about embracing the fire for change. Anyone who truly knows me knows I always have stories. Now this story is a little different because it is written how Milton Erickson would tell his stories. He was an American psychiatrist and psychologist. He specialized in medical hypnosis and family therapy, and his favorite modality was conversational hypnosis. Milton would just tell a story and often the patient would leave confused and not thinking he had done anything. A few days later, they would do something they thought was impossible and not think twice about it.

A man once came to me, deeply frustrated with where his life had led. "I've tried so many things to change," he said, "But every time I start, it feels like I'm walking into a fire. So, I pull back, afraid of getting burned."

I listened for a moment and said, "You remind me of a farmer I knew many years ago. His fields had grown barren over the years, the soil hard and dry. He tried to plant the same crops each season, but nothing would grow. So, he went to an old friend for advice, a man who had worked the land his entire life.

I paused and noticed the man leaning in.

"The friend told him something unusual. He said, 'You need to burn the fields.' The farmer was shocked. Burn the fields? It sounded destructive. Why would he set fire to something he was trying to bring back to life?"

I saw a flicker of understanding in the man's eyes.

"You see," I continued, "What the friend knew is sometimes, fire is necessary. A controlled burn clears away the old, the dead, and the hard, making room for fresh growth. The fire loosens the soil, adds nutrients, and allows the seeds to take root."

The man nodded slowly.

"Now, that farmer didn't set the whole field ablaze all at once. No, he started small, carefully tending the fire, letting it work its way through the dead brush. Over time, the soil became rich again, and in the next season, new crops grew strong and healthy."

I looked at him and said, "Maybe the fire you fear isn't meant to harm you. Maybe it's just there to clear away the old, to soften the ground so that something new can take root. You don't need to fear the flames, just guide them, step by step."

He left, not afraid of the fire, but ready to let it reshape him.

About David King

David King is a transformative coach and the driving force behind King Ventures, specializing in helping Realtors and individuals break through personal and professional barriers. With certifications in Hypnotherapy, Life and Success Coaching, Emotional Freedom Techniques (EFT), and Time Techniques, David offers a powerful blend of tools to guide clients through life-changing challenges such as smoking cessation, weight loss, and overcoming limiting beliefs.

As a Master Hypnotist and Firewalk Instructor, David empowers his clients to face fears, unlock inner strength, and embrace transformation. His holistic approach, combined with expertise as a Master Practitioner of Time Techniques and EFT, allows him to address deep emotional and mental blocks, paving the way for lasting change.

David's compassionate and results-driven coaching style has helped countless individuals realize their potential, achieve their goals, and lead more fulfilling lives.

To receive a gift from David, visit:

www.InnerRevolutionBook.com/gift/David

Inner Revolution: Embracing Change to Achieve Greatness

The Art of Building Rapport
Marcia Souza, NLPP, PTT, CCHt, CSC, EFT

In today's world, connecting with others is important. Being able to build rapport, or a good relationship, helps in many areas, like jobs, friendships, and social situations. Rapport means having a strong and trusting connection with someone. It's more than just getting along; it's about attempting to understand and trust each other. When you get good at building rapport, you can turn simple interactions into meaningful relationships.

One good way to improve communication is to use video calls instead of just text messages. Video calls help you see people's faces and body language, just like in real meetings. This helps build a good connection. It's also important to show that you are paying attention during video calls. You can do this by looking at the camera, nodding your head, and smiling. These simple actions can make a big difference.

Also, you can make a personal connection online by sharing something about yourself and asking others to share, too. Starting meetings with casual talk or fun activities can create a friendly atmosphere. Using interactive tools like polls, breakout rooms, and shared documents can help everyone join in and feel connected. By adjusting regular ways of building friendships to work online, you can make sure your connections stay strong and meaningful, no matter how you communicate.

In this chapter, we will learn what rapport is, how to build it, and why it is important for success in both personal and work life. Whether you're talking to a coworker, a client, a loved one, or even someone you just met, rapport is the key to good relationships. Let's look closer at how to build rapport.

Understanding Rapport

Rapport means making others feel comfortable and connected with you. It's like a silent language that builds trust and teamwork. When you have rapport, talking feels easy, and everyone feels listened to, respected, and important.

Building rapport doesn't happen by chance. It needs effort, understanding, and empathy. Some people think it's just copying someone's body language or tone of voice, but it's more than that. Real rapport comes from mutual respect and feeling like "we are in this together."

A key part of building a good connection is understanding how the other person feels and thinks. To do this, you need to be fully focused on the conversation and show genuine interest in the person you are talking to. By spending time and effort to learn and practice these skills, you can get better at communicating and make a positive difference in the lives of people around you.

The Science Behind Rapport

Research shows that people are made for connection. From an evolutionary view, being able to trust and work together in groups has been important for survival. When we feel close to others, our brains release chemicals like oxytocin. This helps us bond with others and feel less stressed.

This brain response shows how important it is to have good connections with others, both in personal and work relationships. In coaching, for example, having a good connection helps create a safe place where clients can share their problems and feelings. Without this connection, talks might stay shallow, stopping real growth and change.

By learning how to build good relationships, you can have better and more meaningful talks with people. This helps you grow and improve together. Being able to connect well with others is important and helps you deal with social situations better.

Rapport and Neuro-Linguistic Programming (NLP)

NLP is a way of understanding how our thoughts, words, and actions are connected. It looks at how we think, how we talk, and how we act and feel. In NLP, getting along well with others is especially important for good communication. It helps us connect with people and has positive results.

NLP gives us special ways to connect with others. You can use these methods in coaching, therapy, business, and even personal relationships. They help you match the other person's way of talking, body language, and feelings. When done right, building rapport with NLP helps you persuade, understand, and grow together.

The Basics of Building Connections in NLP

1. Pacing and Leading: This technique means matching the other person's words and body language before gently guiding them. By copying how they talk, their tone, and their body movements, you can build a connection. Once you have this connection, you can then guide the conversation in a new direction.

2. Matching and Mirroring: NLP teaches that matching and mirroring are key ways to build a good connection with someone. This means copying the other person's body language, movements, and even how they breathe. When you do this, the other person feels a bond with you without knowing why, making it easier to connect with them.

3. Sensory-Based Language: It's important to notice and respond to how the other person likes to take in information. They might prefer seeing (visual), hearing (auditory), or touching/feeling (kinesthetic). Using the same type of language they use helps build a good connection with them.

4. VAK Modalities: In NLP, it's helpful to know if someone is mainly visual, auditory, or kinesthetic. This can make it easier to connect with them. Use words that match their style (like visual words for visual people) to get along better.

5. Anchoring: Linking a certain action, like a handshake or special phrase, with a feeling can make people feel good and build a strong connection.

Building Good Relationships in Cross-Cultural Communication

In today's world, getting along with people from different cultures is very important. Cultural rules can change how we connect with others. Building good relationships with people from different cultures starts with understanding and respecting their differences. It's important to pay attention to both spoken words and body language, as they may differ from what you're used to. For example, in some places, looking people in the eye shows respect. In other places, it can seem rude. Being curious and wanting to learn about someone else's customs can help make better connections.

Consistently applying these strategies helps us make a lasting positive impression on others. This makes each meeting more than just a chat; it becomes a genuine connection. Using these ideas in your daily interactions not only helps you bond with others, but also creates a kinder and more understanding environment.

Practical Tips:

• Ask Questions: Show curiosity about the other person's culture.

• Adapt Flexibly: Adjust your communication style as needed and remain open to learning.

• Observe Non-Verbal Cues: Pay attention to body language and other cultural gestures to avoid misunderstandings.

Through comprehending and applying these techniques, you can create environments where collaboration and mutual respect thrive, ultimately leading to more productive and harmonious outcomes in various aspects of life.

The Role of Emotional Intelligence (EQ) in Building Rapport

EQ is one of the most crucial skills for building rapport. EQ involves the ability to recognize, understand, and manage your own emotions, while also being attuned to others' emotions. People with high emotional intelligence are naturally better at building rapport because they can read social and emotional cues and adjust their behavior accordingly. By integrating these techniques into your daily interactions, you not only enhance your communication skills but also create an environment where collaboration and mutual respect flourish.

Key Components of EQ:

• Self-Awareness: Helps you remain calm and present in conversations, improving rapport.

• Empathy: Allows you to connect with others by understanding their feelings and perspectives.

• Social Skills: Enable you to find common ground and create a sense of comfort.

- Self-Regulation: Ensures that your emotional reactions don't disrupt rapport building.

Case Studies on Successful Rapport Building

1. Coaching: A life coach used mirroring and active listening techniques to build rapport with a client hesitant to open up. Gradually, the client felt comfortable sharing deeper issues, leading to a revolutionary coaching experience.

2. Business Negotiation: A sales executive established rapport with an international client by adjusting their communication style and finding common ground. This rapport helped close a major deal beneficial to both parties.

3. Therapy: A trauma therapist created rapport with a client by using empathetic listening and pacing. The client, initially resistant, felt safe enough to confront their trauma, leading to a successful therapeutic outcome.

Rapport in Conflict Resolution and Mediation

In conflict resolution, rapport is essential for creating trust and mutual respect, helping to de-escalate emotions and foster cooperation. Without rapport, conflicts often become more difficult to resolve.

Learning and applying these techniques is not an overnight process. It requires consistent practice, self-reflection, and a genuine interest in others. Start by observing your own interactions and identifying areas where you can improve. Pay attention to the subtle cues in body language, tone of voice, and choice of words. Practice active listening, which involves not just hearing the words but understanding the underlying emotions and intentions.

As you become more adept at these skills, you find that building rapport becomes an instinctive part of your daily interactions. This journey towards mastering rapport is not just about enhancing your communication skills; it's about becoming a more empathetic and connected individual.

Techniques for Building Rapport in Conflict Resolution:

• Active Listening: Ensures both parties feel heard, reducing tension.

• Non-Judgmental Approach: Avoids taking sides and help maintain neutrality.

• Addressing Problems from a New Perspective (reframing issues): Helps shift focus from conflict to potential solutions.

Rapport in Team Dynamics and Leadership

Leaders who build rapport with their teams foster a collaborative and high-performing environment. Rapport enhances trust, encourages open communication, and boosts morale.

Ways Leaders Can Build Rapport:

• Personal Check-ins: Regularly touch base with team members on a personal level to show care.

• Empowering Team Members: Support team members' growth by providing resources and encouragement.

- Conflict Mediation: When tensions arise, rapport allows leaders to mediate effectively, ensuring harmony within the team.

The Neuroscience of Rapport

Rapport building is rooted in the brain's neuroscience. Our brains are wired to connect, and certain chemicals, like oxytocin and dopamine, are released during positive social interactions, reinforcing trust and connection.

When we observe others, our mirror neurons fire, enabling us to empathize and imitate their behaviors. This natural response is enhanced by oxytocin, often referred to as the "bonding hormone," which is released during positive interactions, deepening our sense of connection. Additionally, dopamine, the neurotransmitter associated with pleasure and reward, is triggered when rapport is built, reinforcing the joy of meaningful social exchanges. Together, these biological processes create the foundation for strong, positive relationships.

Rapport is not just a transient state, but a continuous process that evolves. The initial efforts in building rapport set the foundation, but maintaining and deepening this connection requires ongoing attention and effort. Regularly engaging in open communication, showing genuine interest, and consistently showing empathy can help sustain rapport in both personal and professional relationships. It's important to remain adaptable and responsive to any changes in the relationship's dynamics, ensuring that the bond remains strong and mutually beneficial.

The Long-Term Benefits of Strong Rapport

Building a strong rapport brings long-term benefits. It enhances personal relationships, fosters professional success, and contributes to overall well-being. Strong rapport reduces conflict, builds loyalty, and fosters deeper trust in both personal and professional interactions.

As we have explored throughout this chapter, building rapport is an essential skill that transcends various aspects of life, from personal relationships to professional environments. Whether through face-to-face interactions or virtual communications, the principles of rapport building remain consistent, yet adaptable to the medium. Techniques such as leveraging video calls, creating personal connections, and using interactive tools are invaluable in maintaining rapport in the digital age.

We delved into the science behind rapport, understanding its neurological foundations, and the critical role emotional intelligence plays in fostering these connections. Techniques from NLP, such as pacing and leading, matching and mirroring, and sensory-based language, provide structured methods to enhance rapport, proving effective across different contexts, including coaching, therapy, and business negotiations. Cultural awareness and emotional intelligence are crucial for building and maintaining rapport, especially in today's globalized world. Their importance cannot be overstated.

The ability to establish and maintain rapport is not just an innate talent, but a skill that can be honed through practice and mindfulness. Engaging in active listening, demonstrating empathy, and showing genuine interest in others are foundational elements that anyone can develop. As you consciously apply these techniques, you'll notice a significant improvement in the quality of your interactions, leading to a more harmonious and productive environment, whether at home or in the workplace. Through mastering the art of rapport building, you open the door to more meaningful interactions and revolutionary relationships, paving the way for both personal and collective growth.

About Marcia Souza

Marcia Souza is a dedicated professional with over 10 years of experience in personal and educational development. As a Certified Practitioner of NLP, Clinical Hypnotherapist, Life and Success Coach, and Parent Coach, she specializes in empowering parents, caregivers, and educators to foster positive relationships with children through innovative techniques.

Marcia holds a Bachelor of Arts in Education from the University of Turabo and has expanded her expertise through certifications in NLP, Hypnotherapy, EFT, and as a Licensed and Registered COSP Facilitator (Circle of Security Parenting based on Attachment Theory). Her comprehensive approach helps individuals reduce stress, enhance productivity, and achieve personal success.

In addition to her coaching practice, Marcia is a co-author of Inner Revolution, underscoring her commitment to empowering education. She is passionate about helping parents build strong, nurturing bonds with their children, ensuring a brighter future for families and communities alike.

Visit her website at www.connectedparentcoaching.net.

To receive Marcia's gift, visit:

www.InnerRevolutionBook.com/gift/Marcia

Through mastering the art of rapport building, you open the door to more meaningful interactions and revolutionary relationships, paving the way for both personal and collective growth.

Inner Revolution: Embracing Change to Achieve Greatness

Inner Revolution: Embracing Change to Achieve Greatness

The Power of Small Steps

Jennifer Altimore, CSC, CCHt

Change is inevitable. You hear that all the time, right? But what if, instead of just hearing it, you could **believe** it, **embrace** it, and **grow** from it?

For me, I learned that change isn't something to fear. Instead, it's something that can lead you to greatness. But change doesn't happen overnight, and it's difficult. It takes work, commitment, and a willingness to dig deep. But the payoff? It's 100% worth it.

My transformation kicked off the moment I tuned into the world of podcasts. Let me give a big shout-out to the plethora of these audio treasures! Tales from real people—navigating struggles that mirror my own—captivated me. Personal finance podcasts became my addiction, and with every episode, I thought, "If they can do it, so can I."

That was my turning point. The more I immersed myself in relatable stories, the stronger my conviction grew in my capacity for change. And let me tell you, that belief was a game-changer.

The more I visualized myself achieving my goals, the more I naturally started working toward them without even realizing it at first. That's the power of belief—it sets everything in motion.

The First Step: Seeing Change as Possible

It all starts in the mind. The mind is incredibly powerful. If you believe change is possible, it will happen. Now, that doesn't mean it'll be easy or that change will magically appear. But belief sets the foundation.

Once I got serious about change, I started writing down my goals. I became obsessed with visualizing what my life would look like once I achieved them. I needed to feel the emotions that those goals I wanted were creating, so I could emulate them on my way to achieving them.

And guess what? It worked. Seeing small bits of progress helped me believe I could achieve even more. It's like momentum: once you see results, it's easier to keep going. Suddenly, the impossible doesn't feel so impossible anymore.

Small Changes, Big Impact

Many people think change has to be monumental to matter. But I've learned that the most lasting change comes from small, consistent steps. I started with simple actions: a two-minute guided meditation from YouTube and writing three things I was grateful for each morning. Nothing complicated or time-consuming, but those small actions snowballed.

Little by little, those habits transformed how I saw the world and, more importantly, how I saw myself. That's the beauty of small steps: they add up. I grew up with big changes—my family moved around a lot, which forced me to adapt quickly.

But the change you have control over, the change you choose, is a lot easier when you break it down into small, manageable steps. It's like climbing a mountain. If you look at the whole thing, it can feel overwhelming. But if you focus on one step at a time, before you know it, you're halfway there.

It's easy to feel like progress is slow and your dreams are out of reach. Have you ever felt stuck, like things aren't moving fast enough? Maybe you've felt defeated because your goals seem so far away. I've been there, too. But when you pause and reflect on all the minor changes you've made, you realize you're not stuck at all. You've been moving forward the entire time. Sometimes, you just need that moment of reflection to see it. And once you do, it fuels you to keep going.

Embracing Resistance: The Sign of Growth

Now, let's talk about resistance—because it's going to show up. It always does, whether it's self-doubt, fear of failure, or negative feedback from others. But here's something I've learned: resistance is a sign you're on the right track. The discomfort you feel when you push through something new is where growth happens. Your brain is rewiring.

When resistance shows up, it's like your mind and body collectively throwing up a caution sign saying, "Are you sure about this? This isn't your usual routine." Instead of retreating, you need to charge ahead.

Self-doubt will always try to sneak in, but I now see it as a golden opportunity. When self-doubt appears, I know I'm on the brink of discovering something new about myself. Ah yes, yet another mindset shift—just like changing your hair color or rearranging your furniture, it's surprisingly effective and will carry you through change with a dash of flair.

Things to Remember About Resistance

To heal, you must first allow yourself to hurt. To genuinely love, you need to break open. And to experience peace, you must face the chaos head-on. These moments of pain and vulnerability are not setbacks, but necessary steps toward balance and growth. There's no light without darkness, no joy without sorrow. It's all a part of the human experience.

I used to think that pain and hardship were things to avoid, but now I see them for what they truly are—building blocks. These experiences bring balance, helping us to heal, learn, and evolve. And through it all, the light always follows.

Here's a little tip on one surefire way to banish self-doubt—positive self-talk with a dash of humor! (Cue entering overly enthusiastic affirmation apps.) Picture this: me striking a superhero pose in front of the mirror, declaring, "I've conquered chaos before, and I can do it again!"

Another little tip..... I even dabble in a little anchoring—no, not the news kind. It's about channeling a past triumph to remind myself that I've got this.

And when the going gets especially tough and I need self-doubt to disappear, I cap off my shower with 30 seconds of

Arctic-level cold water. It's a brisk reminder that if I can endure that, I can handle anything life throws my way.

Dealing with Negative Feedback

Another form of resistance comes from outside—negative feedback from others. In the past, I used to shy away from telling people about my goals because I didn't want to hear my doubts reflected on me by someone else. But I realized something: most people are negative because they're afraid of change themselves. Their fear has nothing to do with you.

When you talk about change, you quickly learn who's on "Team You" and who isn't. Surround yourself with people who lift you and push you forward. If you can't find those people in your immediate circle, look elsewhere. Join groups, clubs, or masterminds with people who are also on their growth journeys. Those people will become your biggest cheerleaders.

Building Habits: Start Small and Stack

Building new habits doesn't have to be hard. One of the easiest ways to create new habits is by stacking them onto existing ones. Let's say you already have a habit of sitting down with your morning coffee and scrolling through your phone. What if you placed a notebook on the table and spent just one minute writing three things you're grateful for? That's all it takes to start a new habit. You're already sitting there—just add in the journaling.

Journaling is powerful for two reasons. First, it helps clear your mind. Getting your thoughts, ideas, or worries out of your head and onto paper is incredibly freeing. Second, it reinforces your goals and desires. When you write something down, you're reinforcing it in your mind. You're thinking about it, writing it, and reading it. That's three times you've planted that idea in your brain. Over time, it becomes part of you.

One of my favorite journaling prompts is: **When I accomplish [goal], I will feel [emotion]. Writing how you want to feel when you reach your goal** keeps you connected to the emotional reward, which helps keep you motivated.

Reflecting on Progress and Celebrating Wins

Reflection is key. It's how you see your growth, even when it feels small. I went through a huge life change after my divorce, and I can easily look back and see the growth in my "pre-D" and "post-D" life. When I look at old pictures or talk to people I haven't seen in a while, I realize just how far I've come. And honestly, I'm proud of where I am. It's not about bragging—it's about acknowledging the work I've put in and celebrating the progress I've made.

There's something truly gratifying about celebrating accomplishments. I love rewards. Setting goals and then treating myself when I achieve them keeps me motivated. Sometimes it's a nice dinner, a new outfit, or a night in the city. It doesn't have to be big, but it should feel special. After all, you deserve to celebrate your wins, no matter how small.

Inner Revolution: Embracing Change to Achieve Greatness

Reframing Setbacks as Lessons

Setbacks are inevitable, but they don't have to derail you. Looking back, some of my biggest challenges turned into my greatest lessons. Shortly after my divorce, everything that could go wrong did. I felt like my world was falling apart. But you know what? I made it through. It was messy and uncomfortable, but it taught me to take things one step at a time.

Nothing worth having comes easily. When you fight for something, it holds greater meaning. That's where the power of reflection comes in—you recognize the strength you didn't know you possessed. And when the next challenge arises, you remind yourself that you've overcome hardships before and ended up leaping forward. So, you do it again... for the leap.

The Power of Belief and Action

Since I've seen the power of change in my life, I now know that **anyone** is capable of it. It all starts in the mind. The mind is incredibly powerful, and as long as you believe change is possible, you can make it happen. It won't be easy, and you'll have to put in the work, but that's what makes it so rewarding.

If you're reading this and feeling like you're on the verge of change, but don't know where to start, I'm here to help. Change can feel overwhelming, but it's always possible. And when you start with small, simple steps, you'll be amazed at how far you can go.

Your next chapter is waiting to be written, one small, powerful step at a time. Start today and let this be the moment that changes everything. Make your next chapter your best one yet!

Checklist for Starting with Small Changes

☐ **Start with One Area of Your Life**

> *Example: Drink an extra glass of water each day*

☐ **Identify Habits You Already Have**

> *Example: While having coffee, add 1 minute of deep breathing*

☐ **Set Small, Achievable Goals**

> *Example: Walk for 10 minutes after lunch each day*

☐ **Track Your Progress**

> *Example: Use a journal or habit tracker app*

☐ **Reward Yourself**

> *Example: Treat yourself after achieving a goal*

About Jennifer Altimore

Jennifer Altimore is a seasoned marketing leader with over 20 years of experience in corporate America, bringing a wealth of knowledge in strategic growth and leadership development.

As the founder of J2ML, LLC, she is a board-certified hypnotist, a life coach, and a student of Neuro-Linguistic Programming (NLP), with a certificate in positive psychology. Jennifer specializes in helping entrepreneurs and business leaders push beyond their comfort zones to reach their fullest potential in business or personal development.

Through her unique blend of corporate expertise, coaching, and mindset transformation tools, she empowers clients to build the life they've always dreamed of, positioning her as a trusted guide for embracing change and achieving greatness.

Get a free gift from Jennifer by visiting:

www.InnerRevolutionBook.com/gift/Jennifer

Inner Revolution: Embracing Change to Achieve Greatness

Inner Revolution: Embracing Change to Achieve Greatness

The Perfectionist's Dilemma - How a Little Mouse Found Bliss Beyond the Boil

Mystral Echavarria, LMT, MHt, MNLP

Let's talk about how much self-love it takes for a mouse to thoroughly enjoy a bowl of pasta for dinner...

Depression is not sadness—most of us know this. To me, it's an experience, not just an emotion.

People can experience those emotions both while depressed and while not depressed. For me, depression was an experience of not knowing what to do with it—a relentless attempt to reject, suppress, or hide from the sadness, anger, hurt, frustration, and overwhelm that I had bubbling out of me all the time.

Imagine a giant boiling pot of water that is constantly bubbling over, and you're a tiny mouse trying to keep that lid on and down, holding on for dear life to the handle as if you were riding a bucking bronco. Trying desperately to keep that lid closed to prevent the water from spilling over...

That's depression—a desperate fight to stay in control, to keep things from boiling over, to stop yourself from falling apart.

And it is exhausting work, my friend.

That's the kind of work that drains your soul. The kind of work that leaves you without anything left to give to yourself.

You end up being pulled in a million different directions, and it feels like no matter how much energy you pour into everything, you're always falling short - especially if you've ever been called or identified as a perfectionist & people-pleaser. Expectations—whether real or imagined—loom large, and when you can't keep up, it all feels like an unending failure.

No wonder we struggle to focus or find joy when it feels like we're just surviving by the skin of our teeth, all while feeling like a mouse holding onto that bubbling pot lid for dear life.

Now, let me tell you how my own pot boiled over...

After my little brother passed away when we were teenagers—I truly felt like I lost a part of my soul that day. While the depression didn't start with the loss of my brother, the build-up after it certainly did. The suppression of emotions did. The heat under my lidded pot got turned way up to HIGH.

Three weeks after his death, I jumped right into college on the other side of the country. I threw myself into it—studying, socializing, having fun, running around NYC like I was unstoppable. On the outside, I looked like I was having the time of my life, but inside I was numb. I had a few grief moments here and there when I couldn't keep it down - and I thought that was enough of an outlet.

My mom & I both had the sense that maybe I hadn't truly dealt with the loss of my brother—that by jumping into college life, by holding desperately onto the mask of being so-called "fine," I had buried my grief, and my body was crying out louder and louder for me to listen to it.

Something clearly had to change. So, I decided to distract myself by taking a year off down in Costa Rica to study massage therapy in the jungle by the beach! Yep, I did that.

Talk about a life-altering decision.

I thought it would be a fun, relaxing escape—a chance to learn something useful and give myself some time to decompress. What I didn't expect was that it would turn into a complete and utter redirection of my entire life. It was no longer just about learning a new skill—but - opening up my awareness to the pain and hurt my body and soul had been trying to yell at me about - but that I had put a wall up and been willingly numb, blind and deaf to before that. Suddenly that wall came down real quick and this experience became all about confronting everything I had been running from for so long. The masks I wore—the "hard worker," the "good girl," the one who at least thought she always held it together—began to feel impossible to maintain.

And through the cracks and openings, came flooding all the emotions I'd held back for so long, uncontrolled, wild, and overwhelming. And I certainly did not know what to do with them. At first, I thought, good, I'm finally letting it all out. But soon, I didn't know how to make it stop.

It just kept coming.

That's when the mouse-on-a-boiling-pot-lid dance really began for me.

You're angry, confused, overwhelmed, and sad. You want to let go, but you're terrified of what might happen if you do. You're clinging on for dear life, because you know if you let go, if that lid pops off, you'll fall and get doused and burned by the boiling-water-overflow of those emotions spilling out everywhere, leaving you curled up on the floor, a sopping, burned, miserable mess.

You begin to wonder to yourself, if you can't do the simple task of keeping the stupid lid on the damn pot, then are you even worth trying to accomplish anything else in life? If I'm just a broken, burned mouse curled up in defeat, am I really contributing anything to the world, or am I just taking up space?

And then, the real kicker that always took it to a whole other level for me: "I wish it had been me instead of my brother - he would have made so much more of this life than I had... It should have been me... It should have been me..." That thought was the one that always plunged me into the whirlpool depths of doom, pain, numbness, and exhaustion. It was completely debilitating.

The way I had always dealt with that was to push through, work harder and hold myself to such a high standard that I often would either freeze from overwhelm and self-criticism or have to recover from burnout and exhaustion.

And despite common & seemingly simple advice like "stop being such a perfectionist," us people-pleasers, end up feeling rather guilty for not being able to figure out how to turn off the illusive perfectionist switch, which makes us then feel like further failures when we can't meet these expectations or follow this advice. We feel like idiots when everyone else seems to be nodding their heads, turning off switches, we're left there still utterly confused and disheartened and wondering what's wrong with us that we can't just figure it out.

To those of you who can relate - no wonder we are always so drained and burned out!

Nevertheless, somehow that little mouse just kept licking her wounds, drying off, and climbing right back onto that lid and she'd start holding on for dear life all over again. And eventually, that little mouse learned some new grips and handholds, new ways to brace herself for landing, finally gave in to dropping some of the masks that were making it hard to see and stepped out of the armor that was weighing her down. She built out some padding and protection for when inevitably the lid would pop off and it would all boil over again - but this time, without the masks that were making it hard to see and without the armor holding in the heat and making it hard to react quickly enough - this time, she didn't get burned.

In fact, she did that cool 007 roll, and landed on her feet this time.

In other words, she didn't give up.

The reason our little mouse began to tear away those masks and armor was that she finally saw them for what they really were—heavy, protective layers that initially were meant to keep her "safe" but that now weighed her down and made things worse by soaking up the boiling water, making it even harder to be agile, so she'd end up clumsily tumbling down painfully, instead of jumping off to safety with ease like she was slowly starting to learn how to do.

And for me, the masks had kept me from seeing clearly so that I could never grasp the big picture—they kept me focused on keeping up the facade on the outside while continuously being drained by barely surviving on the inside. As I removed the masks and the armor, little by little, I gained more agility, the ability to experiment more playfully with moving through life without all that cumbersome armor weighing me down.

Tearing away the masks was like taking off a blindfold. Suddenly, I could see options I hadn't seen before - like therapy, like asking for help, like exploring the power of skilled and intentional bodywork and energy work that could help train me how to find my way back that place of peace in my mind and body faster and more consistently no matter what ups, downs and adventures life throws my way.

Without the masks clouding my vision, I could start to see and hear what I really wanted, and everything began to shift.

I could see that I didn't have to do it all alone, and I didn't need to keep pretending.

I didn't need to be "fine" or "not a burden" to be loved.

I didn't need to bottle up my emotions to be accepted.

I even learned that I could let the pot boil over if I needed to.

I could turn down the heat.

I could step away from the lid entirely and just observe it.

And here's the really cool part about that—When you can surrender into your peek-a-boo moments of clarity, you begin to see flashes of different possibilities and different paths. Even never knowing when that depression cycle will start up again, you start to make the most out of whatever moments of joy & and bursts of pleasure you can get, you start to build resilience and you start to demand ease, flow and respect for yourself, little by little, more and more, from others, and most importantly from yourself..

Now, are there much less painful ways of building resilience?

Yes absolutely.

But I've never been one to take the easy route, have I?

What I have done, in all my experimentation, is pulled together the shortcuts, so you don't have to. And so, one day, after years of said experimentation with pot boiling and tearing away masks and armor little by little, came a moment of profound clarity—one I vividly remember. I was in my apartment after sending an energy healing session to a client who was going through a tough time.

I had just finished grounding myself when suddenly, I felt like I was way up high, soaring through the night sky, feeling the wind in my hair. And I saw little glowing green lights, representing the souls of all the people sprinkled across the landscape down below me. Just as I had sent love and support to my client, only minutes earlier, I also had this urge to send my love to everyone - to all the little green lights as far as I could see!

And so I did.

Some received it and glowed brighter, others rejected it, and that was okay.

And I started refining this new experience of sending love in this way, because I started to realize that some of the green lights received my love, but they also took hold, and drained me until I had to tear myself away.

So I told my heart to only send my beams of love to those whom it would be in the highest good for both of us.

And that felt much better. I was no longer having to give up so much of myself. And that was when I felt a shift—an ease, a lightness - I was actually feeling really charged up! I was giving without draining myself, which was honestly a new sensation for me.

Then I had an idea—what if I sent love to myself as well? So I decided to test out an experiment. This time, every time I sent a beam of light out to a little green glowing soul down below, I also sent a second beam looped back around to myself as well. Just imagine as I was soaring over the Eastern seaboard, how many green glows below I was seeing and that many times over I was both sending & receiving that amount of love in a sort of infinite love loop to myself!?

Can you see it?

Can you feel it?

Can you do that for yourself?

Because let me tell you how well I slept that night after I brought my awareness back into my body. All I can say is the next morning, I woke up and something was different. It took a little while before I remembered that it was the anniversary of my brother's death, and for the first time in over a decade, I was truly and honestly fine ... I was even feeling a little light and happy; peaceful and grateful..... and then it hit me!

My depression was completely gone. This ever-present weight I'd learned to live with for years - It just wasn't there anymore. Mind you, I had spent years going to therapy, doing a lot of self-exploration, and deep energy work, and introspective healing and learning and growing leading up to this.

But that journey with the infinite love loop and green lights is what really closed out that particular chapter for me.

And I can't help but feel, given the timing, that my brother had at least a small guiding hand in helping me get there that night. And that, of course, fills my heart and makes me smile.

It was honestly a bit of an identity crisis. Because now I finally had the energy and capacity to explore new and lit up paths meant just for me that I had been seeking out so desperately for years, but had been blind to before.

Imagine what life could look like without the constant drain of indecision and guilt. Picture the energy you'd have—not just to meet expectations, but to chase after the things you truly want. Imagine the ripple effect that would create in your relationships, your communities, and within yourself. And just imagine the freedom that could come if, instead of tipping our cups to pour endlessly into others, we allowed them to fill up to overflowing.

Imagine that fullness spilling naturally into the people we want to serve, the projects we've kept on the back burner, and the dreams we've quietly shelved, ready to come to life once and for all. Just imagine how amazing that would be…

So tell me, in that maybe not so imaginary world, what does the little mouse do with herself, now that she's finally learned to let go, shed the masks, and embrace what truly lights her up? Perhaps now that the little mouse is no longer fighting to keep a lid on a boiling pot of water, she can finally sit down with a delicious glass of wine and truly enjoy a scrumptious pasta dinner.

About Mystral Echavarria

Mystral Echavarria is a Somatic Energy Healer, Hypnotist, and Intuitive Life Coach with 17+ years of experience. She is the creator of Practical Woo™, a holistic approach blending grounded strategy with shamanic intuitive wisdom to support mind, body, and soul.

As a Master Practitioner in Neuro-Linguistic Programming, Neuromuscular Therapy, Compassion Key and Timeline Therapy, Mystral helps visionary perfectionists and people-pleasers who are tired of getting in their own way and who are finally ready to go after what has always felt just out of reach and that has stayed on the back burner for far too long.

Mystral reignites her clients' bold, unstoppable energy, ensuring they feel held and motivated to soar beyond their up-till-now limitations. Her clients arrive feeling disconnected and overwhelmed, but leave with renewed confidence, clarity, and full of excitement to wake up and roar to life.

When she's not helping clients step into their full power, you'll find her biking through the streets of NYC, dancing her heart out, and dreaming of her next scuba adventure.

Get a free gift from Mystral by visiting:

www.InnerRevolutionBook.com/gift/Mystral

Inner Revolution: Embracing Change to Achieve Greatness

The Victorious Secret Sauce
Dawn Aldredge, MNLP, MTT, MHt, MSC, and Trainer of NLP

Have you ever felt like you were drowning in quicksand, as if the walls of "too muchness" were closing in around you? I was amazed when I finally realized that the bottomless pit that resulted in this overwhelming feeling, stemmed from a belief that nothing was ever "good enough".

"Shame loves perfectionists. It's so easy to keep us quiet." ~Brene Brown

As a kid, I had a phenomenal skill set with lightning speed and incredible potential for playing soccer. Soccer was exhilarating to me. I can still remember the smell of that freshly cut grass on those cool September mornings. I loved the feeling of being in the zone.

Unfortunately, I developed a habit while under pressure where I would freeze up when the opportunity arose to take a shot. Most kids would seize the opportunity, sprinting toward the goal & with just a few cuts, place the ball in the net.

Me? When the opportunity to score presented itself, my heart rate suddenly shot through the roof as my breathing became shallow. Unable to control my racing heart, a cold sweat enveloped me as I stood there frozen. I felt humiliated for others to see me lose control over my mind & body.

As I stood there panic stricken, I had no power to take the shot. I had to pass the ball.

In those moments, my spirit felt crushed for being "the one" to let the team and the fans down. Anger led me to engage in harsh self-talk, blaming and shaming myself for yet another disappointing performance.

My fear strengthened as I worried about the next time I would choke again.

Time and again, I swear I was hearing my mother's voice saying, "How dare you think you are good enough to take that shot?"

Mom kept a flawless house that she ran like a totalitarian dictatorship.

For some reason Mom had to keep a tight grip over every move I made, every morsel I ate, and every breath I took.

One day, she forced me sit at the dinner table for about 30 minutes, chewing on a grizzly piece of chuck that was too large to swallow without choking. The pressure to live up to Mom's expectations to swallow that enormous tough piece of meat left me feeling completely helpless.

I was damned if I swallowed it and damned if I didn't. I was in a double bind. Ironically, if I had done as she told me to do, I would have choked! My dad finally stepped in and told her to cut it out.

This constant micromanagement occurred so frequently that when I became an adult, I would quit & submit to my circumstances whenever I stumbled over a trigger of those childhood "double bind" memories.

 Finding myself under pressure to meet others' expectations, I would lose all motivation to try at all.

"Perfectionism doesn't make you feel perfect. It makes you feel inadequate." ~Maria Shriver

By adulthood, every single day was a battleground obsessing about how to best micromanage my eating, my body weight & my appearance while overachieving to meet extraordinary expectations all to prove I was good enough. I was extremely overcritical of myself.

I believed my value was tied directly to my appearance, popularity & achievements. I was driven to win this game of extraordinary perfection at all cost. I spent time at the regular gym motivated mostly to invest in my looks.

After my second marriage ended I was forced to figure out how to survive on my own. Mom ended up going to bed one day, and decided to never get back up again. I watched as she descended into the depths of decrepitude. Now that I found myself alone, I was driven to make sure I did not end up like Mom.

I learned about the growth mindset in 2015 when I became a real estate agent at Keller Williams Realty. Gary Keller quotes were the foundation with which I built my new life.

At about the same time I became a Real Estate agent I joined a CrossFit gym nearby. Ironically, this specific gym seemed to teach many of those same growth mindset principals I read in those Gary Keller books such as "the one thing." The director at that CrossFit gym was a champion at setting boundaries, telling mindset shifting metaphors & saying no amongst many other things. I had never seen anyone set boundaries and say no like that guy did. I was fascinated to see how he did it because I had a feeling that as a new real estate agent this boundary setting thing was something I needed to learn, pronto!

He was exceptionally skilled at creating a fun exhilarating atmosphere where we could invest in soul-shifting sweat drenching workouts within his community. I looked forward to doing those workouts again and again. I was so motivated to show up at this place and workout as a form of fun, rather than stand there in the mirror admiring my own looks as in the past.

I also found it strangely interesting that in addition to his champion level boundary setting & story telling, he was rewarding our effort, rather than only rewarding the extraordinary results.

This was crazy to me. I had always been extraordinary results-driven because even extraordinary was rarely "enough." Unlike this guy, my self-confidence was connected to my results. My achievements needed to be "over" achievements at all cost. Being an average passing "C" achiever was grounds for a major do-over.

"It's not over when you lose, it's over when you quit."

I was so happy with how my mindset was shifting at this new exhilarating fun fitness gym that I asked him if I could do a showcase video there to highlight all the benefits of how that gym experience changes lives.

He said no. I continued on and asked him again about a year later. He said no again.

And then, after showing him some work I had done for local businesses that came out pretty good, I asked yet again. Finally, he entertained me and said yes.

Suddenly, the pressure rose. Astonishingly, I didn't feel like I could measure up. He had real confidence. I backed myself into a corner, having to face the fact that I had false confidence. I was a fake!

After the excitement of receiving pre-approval from so many local people who were thrilled about the video wore off, I choked.

I couldn't take the shot and instead sabotaged myself. I then placed my tail between my legs and put the thought of it off for a long time, actually hoping he would simply forget. After lots of time went by, he realized I would not do it. I felt extremely low letting everyone down after it took so long to get that YES.

Learning from Failure and Moving Forward

I continued self-validating my tiny wins & effort on my own after I moved on from that gym family. There was something very magical that was happening for me by simply validating my tiny wins. That self validation turned into self motivation. This eventually turned out to be the underlying key to a Champion level mindset that freed my true authentic self as I built a foundation of genuine self-confidence.

Change is inevitable, growth is optional

It was 2018 & with multiple offer hell running the show, Real Estate was no longer cutting the mustard for me with that level of stress. I wanted to do something more fulfilling. I decided I wanted to teach self motivation in order to change lives the way my life began to change at that first CrossFit Gym.

I became a personal fitness trainer and quickly took an internship at a local regular gym. I was shocked how at the regular local gym many of the members struggled with motivation and behavior modification. As It turned out, that struggle with behavior modification and motivation was very close to my own struggle.

After the gyms closed up when COVID rolled in, I set out on a quest to find the secret behind self motivation. I needed to understand why I was so motivated to do those CrossFit workouts, as well as find the secret behind behavior modification so that I could share this formula with my fitness clients.

There was something about the barbell movements at that first CrossFit gym that ramped up the intensity for me to an exhilarating level like nothing else I had ever known. I was convinced that was what my unmotivated gym clients needed in order to learn self motivation. I decided to invest in attending the CrossFit Coaches training so that I could learn how to cue the barbell movements.

Of the many skills to learn through investing in CrossFit, the only one I was a master of five years later, was the basic push up. For some reason I was unable to get motivated enough to stick with a practice schedule in order to learn any of the other movements such as the double under which is an exciting skill where the rope spins twice under your feet.

It seemed as if mostly everyone else knew how to do the double under except for me. I tried for years & years to master the skill and as the rope tangled up around me and bruised up my shins, I would quit time and time again in frustration. When asked about it, I kept saying "I can't do the double under".

Eventually, I thought to myself "how will I ever be able to be a CrossFit Coach teaching classes if I am unable to master just this one skill?

Inner Revolution: Embracing Change to Achieve Greatness

"The revolution begins within"

During my quest to find the victorious secret sauce to self motivation & behavior modification I had read the book "Becoming Supernatural" by Dr. Joe Dispenza. I began to do some of the meditations in the book as well as the visualizations. To my delight, my life began to swiftly shift in a new empowered direction.

I found Rapid Transformational Therapy after doing an internet search on hypnotic words that I could add to Dr. Joe D's meditations. I then signed up for RTT and learned all about the hypnotic words, dialogue with the subconscious mind, as well as the rules of the mind.

At the same time that I signed up for RTT, I signed up for NLP & Life Force Energy Healing. I was convinced I was very challenged due to the complications of complex post traumatic stress disorder and needed a higher level of consciousness to be able to fully overcome it hence the energy healing. Through RTT, NLP & Life Force Energy Healing I learned very much about flow states, synchronicity and overcoming resistance to maintain alignment.

"Grace means that all of your mistakes now serve a purpose instead of serving shame."

~Brene Brown

After some time of investing in that mindset upgrade trifecta, I was delighted to finally be able to find out why I was unable to be motivated enough to regularly practice in order to learn the double under skill for so long.

Over this time investing in upgrading my mindset, I became very self aware of the way I spoke to myself. I tuned into the fact that I had been repeatedly saying to myself, I MUST do the double under. Believe it or not words are magical and that is why they call it spelling. The word MUST used in my inner dialogue was placing me in a state of FORCE. Being in a state of force meant I was in resistance. And when in the "state" of resistance I would automatically quit and submit losing all motivation. This was occurring beyond my conscious control. It was similar to those double bind memories that occurred with Mom's force feeding, over-control and micromanagement.

Being in a state of force using the word MUST, meant I was being motivated by the applause of the crowd. This was rather than being intrinsically motivated by wanting to perform for myself. This "one thing" was the key to overcome not only the resistance that prevented me from doing the double under, additionally this was the key to overcoming the self sabotage that would occur when under pressure to perform.

The kicker to this whole dilemma was that before I could release the resistance, I had to literally validate for myself that "I am good enough" as I was completely basic, without the extraordinary skill or the extraordinary body or the extraordinary performance. I had to be sure I was ENOUGH all on my own as an ordinary passing C. Otherwise I was unable to escape from the self sabotage that would result due being externally motivated.

I created a system to learn the double under skill over an 8 week period. I committed to 5 minutes per day, every single day of showing up regardless of how ugly or beautiful the practice went. I used the growth mindset by telling myself "I do not have the double under, YET" rather than saying "I can't do the double under". Additionally, every day I said to myself several times, "I am so excited to learn the double under, all for me."

As the momentum of each day of practice got rolling, I started to look forward to practicing. I was training my mind at a neuroplastic level to be self motivated. At the point where I was so frustrated that I didn't have even one double under YET, I reminded myself to have FAITH in the unseen, because I knew that the moment I wanted to quit was the moment that success was right around the corner.

When I finally got my rhythm after about 8 weeks of consistent practice, I was able to string together about 3 double unders in a row.

As a result of the system that I created to learn that skill, I learned to believe in myself & became a self empowered self motivator. To this day, whenever I get stuck with any of life's challenges where the temptation to quit overwhelms me, I refer back to that double under system I created for self motivation in order to remind myself of how I succeeded on my own in the past.

After moving on and continuing to model that original CrossFit gym director's Champion level growth mindset, maladaptive Perfectionism, demotivation, performance anxiety & a debilitating case of Complex Post Traumatic Stress disorder are mostly now behind me.

I am proud of myself to now be persevering to the end.

About Dawn Aldredge

Dawn Aldredge is a Peak Performance Coach dedicated to helping athletes and high-performing professionals achieve peak performance through flow mastery. As a personal fitness trainer, she integrates high-intensity workouts with concepts from the growth mindset and Neuro-Linguistic Programming (NLP) to elevate neurochemical states, facilitating swift shifts toward desired outcomes.

Dawn conducts workshops on NLP, Rapid Transformational Therapy, and Life Force Energy Healing, empowering participants to become their own growth mindset coaches and fostering self-reflection to share with others.

She is a Certified Trainer of NLP, a Certified Trainer of Clinical Hypnotherapy, a Personal Fitness Trainer, a CrossFit Level 1 Coach, an Irest Yoga Nidra Teacher, a Level 5 Life Force Energy Healing Practitioner, and a Rapid Transformational Therapy Practitioner and Coach.

For more information, visit www.dawnaldredge.com

Get Dawn's gift, go to:

www.InnerRevolutionBook.com/gift/Dawn

"Grace means that all of your mistakes now serve a purpose instead of serving shame."

~Brene Brown

Inner Revolution: Embracing Change to Achieve Greatness

The PAWS Method: Purpose-Driven Outcomes, Alignment, Walk the Walk, and Study

Rachel Bock, CSC, CCHt

As a software developer, I program behaviors. There are expected behaviors we want the program to do. And then, there are unexpected behaviors. In order to isolate what behaviors are expected and desired, we look for patterns and examine the results of the program. If I give the program certain inputs, what are the expected outputs? What are the actual outputs I received? Are the outputs the same? If not, how are they different and why?

T. Harv Eker teaches our thoughts lead to our feelings. Our feelings lead to our actions. And our actions lead to our results. We can control our thoughts, feelings, and actions. Through these three, we can indirectly control our results. I'll summarize that as "Thoughts + Feelings + Actions = Results."

Michael Stevenson teaches that there are multiple layers of the mind. The most influential being our identities followed by our values, beliefs, and so on. Using this information and the Eker formula described above, let's look at how software development's iterative process can help us embrace change and create the results we seek.

Actually, that's the first of the six *Principles for Success* taught by Michael Stevenson and Transform Destiny. "<u>Know</u> your outcome," or what results you seek. Just like there are requirements in software development, you need to know what behavior or results you want. For Neuro-Linguistic Programming (NLP) purposes, to know an outcome is more than just being able to describe it. Knowing your outcome is more than just having a vague idea of what you want to have happen.

Knowing the outcome includes seeing, hearing, and feeling the outcome as if it's happening now, first from the perspective of seeing from your own eyes and then from the perspective of seeing yourself in the visualization doing, having, or being in the desired outcome.

The second principle for success is to "Take **real** <u>action</u>." When Michael discusses this principle for success, he asks, "What is the bare minimum that you can commit to do 100% no matter what?" Small steps can take you further through the greatest journey than the best of intentions.

Principal three is "Pay attention to your <u>results</u>." When you pay attention to your results, you want to ask, "Is this moving me toward my desired outcome, or is it moving me away from my desired outcome?" Keep in mind, it's not about success or failure. It's not about good or bad. It is about whether you move toward or away from the outcome.

Principal number four is "Be willing to <u>change</u> your behavior." Many times, when I've heard or seen Michael present this principle, he will say something to the effect that he would change the principle. Instead of saying be willing to change your behavior, he would have it as "Be willing to change." Sometimes it is a behavior that needs to change. However, based on the layers of the mind, there are more foundational parts that may need to change. You may need to change how you see yourself or what's important to you.

Principal number five is "Always focus on <u>excellence</u>." You don't have to be perfect. Instead, focus on giving your best. This reminds me of the question "Am I better today than I was yesterday?" Excellence is not only a continual improvement and growth. It is also personal. Your best may vary from day to day. Make sure your personal best is improving overall.

Principal number six is to "Live life with <u>gratitude</u> and <u>integrity</u>." Michael's definition of integrity is threefold. First, say what you mean. Second, do what you say. And third, always seek win-win outcomes. Or, in other words, take care of others. Also, to live with gratitude includes being grateful for your challenges. Recognize that the challenge is here to help you grow.

Just like the first principle of success, the first step in the PAWS method is to have a purpose-driven outcome. When I use 'purpose-driven' here, I'm using it to refer to a North Star, big picture outcome. Specifically, what is it we want to achieve? For programming, I want specific behaviors from the software. Before I touch the codebase, I want to know what the expected behavior is going to produce. I write automated tests that give me a feel for whether that behavior is working the way I want it to. At the beginning, these tests fail because there is no code to make the tests pass. I want them to fail to let me know that when they pass, the code suffices to produce the desired behavior.

Similarly, in real life, I want specific results. For example, like so many of us, I struggle with my weight. My purpose-driven outcome may be to become healthier. "To become healthier" may sound like a logical outcome, and it is for some people. However, the subconscious mind needs specific and clear instructions. Healthier than what? Healthier than today? Will that ever happen if it is always today?

I can use the NLP method of creating an outcome to establish the result I seek more clearly. I can more clearly specify what my purpose is in the actions that I will be taking. In regular goal setting philosophies, we use SMART goals to define the desired outcome. And in NLP, there is a similar acronym with additional context for how to set a desired outcome.

When working with my coaching clients, I like to use a technique that helps identify not only the desired outcome but also (1) when they want an outcome to exist in their life, (2) what they see, feel and hear when they know they have reached that outcome as well as (3) the personal intangible resources that they have that will help them move towards this purpose-driven outcome.

When defining a purpose-driven outcome, many people have one of two common issues. There may be a lack of commitment. When I say "commitment," I mean the ability to accomplish what one said they would do, no matter what. It's the "no matter what" that seems to fall apart sometimes.

Second, many people don't know what resources they have that can really move the needle. When this happens, I ask my clients to visualize someone they know who could accomplish the desired outcome. What resources would that person have and use to accomplish the outcome?

Once we have committed to a purpose-driven outcome and have a clear direction, next, we need to be in alignment in order to move towards this purpose. When I say "alignment," I mean how we see ourselves, what we value as important, and what we believe will dictate how we behave and what actions we choose to use in order to move us towards (or away) from that purpose-driven outcome. An example of being out of alignment is when we say we want something, and our actions move us away from that outcome. This is how I recognize that something isn't adding up.

In software development, knowing the outcome and the expected behavior and the current behavior gives me a way to know what needs to change. It gives me a direction that I can use to know how to change the existing behavior to get the desired results. I primarily use testing to ensure that the desired behavior is accomplished. I'll come back to testing in a later step.

The third step is to "walk the walk." Do the actions that will bring results. For programming, this step is where I put the code into place. I add the logic to create the desired behavior. Here's where it gets iterative. I add the code, then check the tests to see if the behavior is what I want. If it isn't, I go back to the code and repeat the process.

Similarly, in life, we are taking action to create the consequences. If I am in alignment, these actions will move me towards my purpose-driven outcome. If not, however, there may be some misalignment to be resolved. The only way to know what the consequences are compared to our desired outcome is to make time to study the results.

When I say, "to study the results," I'm talking about step four; thinking deeply about what thoughts and feelings went into my actions and what results appeared because of those thoughts, feelings, and actions. Ask questions. Ponder responses to those questions.

For me, the most powerful questions aren't the why questions. It is actually how and what questions that can move me forward. This is where testing comes in. The tests we use as developers are either/or tests. They either are giving us the behaviors we want, or they aren't. They pass or fail. It's a yes/no proposition. There is not maybe. Either the behavior is meeting expectations, or it isn't there yet.

Let's talk more about testing. In *Test Driven Development*, for *Red-Green testing*, the tests are set up before any coding is done. All the tests fail because there isn't any code implemented yet to produce the desired behavior. When tests are created, we have a specific testing strategy that includes these yes/no types of tests. Automated tests will look at the responses from a function and determine if the response matches what is expected

When the development process begins, the tests are "red." They don't pass. There are unmet expectations. As development takes place, some tests begin to "go green." Some tests will match expectations and are then considered passing tests. When all tests are green, development can stop because the desired behavior has been accomplished.

But what about this testing that makes it work so effectively? It's because we test everything. We test when things work and when things don't work. Then we intentionally break the tests to make sure that they are testing what they need to. We test the tests.

How does this apply to reaching our desired outcomes? As discussed earlier, Michael's Principles for Success includes "Be willing to change." As I mentioned, being overweight is a struggle for me. It is unhealthy for me. However, in order to change my physical weight, I would want to change my thoughts, feelings and actions that are causing me to be a specific weight. With weight, I can change what I eat and how often I exercise. Is that enough?

Not necessarily. I want to make a permanent change. As such, I want to see myself as healthy and active. I want to stand at my work desk instead of sitting all day, valuing my health and strength. I want to have beliefs that are in alignment with these identities and values, believing that being healthy is possible for me.

These identities, values, and beliefs will influence my actions when I'm deciding between that last piece of birthday cake and the carrots sitting in the fridge. Being in alignment will help me when I am choosing to watch a movie from the couch or on the treadmill.

"Be willing to change" isn't just about doing something different. It's about being or becoming different. For example, with my weight, being willing to change means being loving to myself, valuing health, and physical strength, and believing that taking care of my body is important to me and that it is possible for me to have a healthy body.

When I use the iterative PAWS method coupled with Micheal's *Principles for Success*, I can more clearly see ways where I have the power to make the changes necessary to reach my purpose-driven outcomes. Years ago, I woke up one morning crying. In my dream, I could not change. It shattered my heart. I felt so imprisoned because of not having the power to change who I was or to change my circumstances. To this day, I have held onto that experience and remembered my gratitude when I was reminded it was only a dream.

My intent is for you to learn that anything is possible. You can change and become the person you want to be. You can live the life you want to live. Much like the first step in any journey is difficult, the hardest part may be to decide how or what that life looks like.

As you may expect, there may be obstacles to overcome. There are also resources available to you that you may not see or be aware of yet. Over time and with practice, the PAWS method, along with the *Principles for Success*, will allow you to have power in your life and accomplish those purpose-driven outcomes and more.

So, I ask you to contemplate, "What is your purpose-driven outcome?" What is it you want?

About Rachel Bock

Rachel Bock is a dedicated Software Development Engineer with experience in Success and Life Coaching. She holds a Bachelor of Science in Mathematics from the University of Colorado, where she graduated cum laude, and has further honed her skills with a Front-End Engineering Certification from the Turing School of Software and Design. She has also deepened her knowledge of personal development and self-mastery through Transform Destiny.

With a passion for helping others, Rachel adapted Transform Destiny's Principles for Success into the memorable PAWS method, an iterative framework designed to help people cultivate and enjoy a purpose-driven life. Her diverse background in software engineering, hypnotherapy, and coaching allows her to blend technical proficiency with holistic personal development strategies.

Rachel is often found satisfying her thirst for knowledge. Besides spending time with family and friends, she enjoys inspiring others to discover their higher purpose and helping them navigate their unique journeys toward fulfillment and success.

To receive Rachel's gift, visit:

www.InnerRevolutionBook.com/gift/Rachel

"Be willing to change" isn't just about doing something different. It's about being or becoming different.

Inner Revolution: Embracing Change to Achieve Greatness

Inner Revolution: Embracing Change to Achieve Greatness

Embracing Vulnerability for Lasting Love
Becky Parker, NLPP, PTT, CCHt, CSC, Mindset Expert

It was a warm summer evening, with the golden hues of the setting sun casting a soft, inviting glow. A slight breeze took the edge off the typical California heat. My new boyfriend, just a few months in, knocked at the door, ready for our usual Friday night date.

I was completely into him—like a squirrel in a peanut butter factory—full of nonstop energy and wide-eyed excitement! I felt good and looked even better in my black tank with lace trim, black leather pants, and my cutest black stilettos. As I strutted my "red carpet walk" to his car, I felt grateful for this wonderful man: a successful business owner who was generous, loving, and supportive.

But just 15 minutes into the drive to the restaurant, an aching feeling hit my stomach, like the sudden drop of a rollercoaster. My mind raced with fears: "I'm going to get screwed over," "Another man who will cheat on me," "Did he flirt with anyone today?" "Does he see me as worthy enough to be his only woman?" These questions haunted me.

Then, as if on cue, I picked a fight. I turned to him and asked, "Do you ever think about other women?" His exasperated look and tone spoke volumes as he reminded me, that I was "it" for him—the lover, buddy, and companion he had been waiting for his whole life. We engaged in a back-and-forth exchange, me intensely questioning while he responded with empathy and patience.

I became visibly agitated, angry, and overwhelmed. Finally, he asked, "WHY are you so angry?" I was left speechless, gazing out the window, grappling with the question of where my anger was coming from.

As we pulled into the valet, a stress-relieving cigarette rested between my lips, ready to be lit at the first chance. My boyfriend, perfectly in stride beside me, dropped the bombshell: "We need to talk."

Inside, over a strong vodka and coke, I listened as he declared his unwavering love, comforting me about my fears. However, he explained he couldn't keep enduring the cycle of my suspicions, skepticism, anger, and distrust. "How about we have a session with my life coach to help with these struggles?" he suggested. In typical Becky fashion, I replied, "You're just trying to brainwash me."

Moments after those words left my lips, I realized that this very mindset was what he meant. I was on the verge of losing someone wonderful unless I changed my thinking. I also recognized I couldn't tackle this challenge alone. Despite countless attempts to manage my swirling thoughts, I remained trapped in a cycle of unhappiness, striving to fill a void within me—a small black hole that never seemed to get filled.

To provide context, my upbringing was rooted in "mind over matter" and "where there's a will, there's a way." Therapy was taboo, reserved for those with significant "issues." So, when the person I loved suggested I talk to someone, I felt conflicted. It clashed with my ingrained beliefs about self-reliance and personal strength. Gratefully, I trusted my boyfriend enough to know I wanted a future with him. Despite my hesitation, I was "unwillingly" willing to go, if only to appease him.

A New Path to Understanding

The following week, we had our appointment with the life coach. During the session, I openly revealed the issues I believed contributed to my relationship struggles: I've been battling an eating disorder since I was 15. If I didn't have the perfect body, I wasn't loveable.

I grew up with the belief men always want sex. Sex is a duty. The man is to start sex. The frequency of sex determines the health of the relationship. Being slutty, even for your husband, is dirty. I am overly judgmental of others, sometimes controlling, with significant trust issues. "What is wrong with me?" was the next sentence out of my mouth.

What the life coach said next was something I had only experienced or heard from one other person in my life: the man sitting beside me. He said, "That's ok! You've developed some strategies to deal with past pain and experiences in your life and we are going to get you unburdened from them!" Wait... what? That was it? No judgment like "What the hell is wrong with you?" I wasn't broke. I didn't need to be "fixed"?

Things progressed quickly and before I knew it, I was taking part in the most profound relationship exercise I had ever experienced. This exercise saved me from inadvertently sabotaging a relationship with the person I considered the greatest man on earth.

My boyfriend and I stood at opposite corners of the room and as we answered each question, the life coach asked, if we would take a step closer to one another. I saw the tears welling in my boyfriend's eyes and could *see, hear,* and *feel* how much he loved me. He would not screw me over. He wasn't in this for false motives.

At that moment, I told myself, "I need to get my shit taken care of." And from that day forward, the life coach was now MY life coach as well.

Revisiting Beliefs for Personal Transformation

During childhood and throughout our personal life experiences, we encounter various messages that we interpret through our unique filters. This process leads us to assign specific meanings to these messages. Over time, we adopt these interpretations as core beliefs and carry them forward as guiding principles in our lives.

These core beliefs, often formed subconsciously, can significantly influence our behaviors, relationships, and overall outlook on life, sometimes without us even realizing it. Recognizing and understanding these core beliefs can be the first step toward transforming them, allowing us to reshape our perceptions and open ourselves to healthier, more fulfilling relationships.

By identifying and challenging these ingrained beliefs, we create opportunities for personal growth and healing, paving the way for deeper connections and a more authentic way of living. This realization marked a pivotal moment in my journey, as I came to understand that acknowledging and addressing these beliefs could lead to profound personal transformation.

As the weeks and months unfolded, my journey with my life coach continued, and I felt a sense of pride in the changes I was making. I dedicated myself to the work of uncovering my truest self, identifying the root causes of my pain, and finding peace and freedom from the beliefs I had formed about myself as a woman. The unhealed child within me felt worthy and good enough.

I recognized my value, understanding that my awesomeness as a woman was not determined by having the "perfect body" or the number on the scale. Not every man was out to screw me over. The man I was in a relationship with wasn't trying to control me. My body wasn't flawed. I was lovable.

Each day, I embraced my newfound sense of self-worth, realizing that true empowerment stems from within, not from external validation. But my healing journey was far from over; it was an ongoing process of self-discovery that required patience, compassion, and a willingness to confront the uncomfortable truths of my past.

In a matter of eight months, I graduated from his girlfriend. To the fiancé. To wife. And let me tell you, the first years of marriage were tumultuous! It was like being on a rollercoaster in the middle of a hurricane—wild ups and downs, twists I didn't see coming, and no way to catch my breath. The scene was filled with chaos: screams echoed, verbal fights broke out, and misunderstandings abounded. Whatever turmoil you could imagine, it was present.

Navigating Turmoil: The Realities of Marriage

After the wedding, I believed I had uncovered and healed my past pain, so I let my virtual sessions with my life coach taper off. Big mistake. Emotions come in layers, and you can never predict when unresolved feelings will resurface. It didn't take long for me to realize that my marriage was bringing to light issues I hadn't fully addressed, pushing me to explore my emotional landscape and confront the hidden layers of my past.

In my mind, I was a brilliant wife—keeping a tidy home, flirting with my husband, cooking hot meals, and supporting his dreams as if they were my own. Yet beneath this facade of domestic bliss lingered insecurities and fears that seeped into our relationship. Each argument felt like a trigger, revealing more emotional baggage than I hadn't unpacked. I realized I wasn't the wife my husband needed; my love language didn't align with his.

My husband craved tenderness and intimacy, an openness that showed my passion and acceptance of him as part of me. Yet I struggled to provide that, fearing and resisting it. Why couldn't he just appreciate what I was already doing? I wasn't made to be demonstrative or overly affectionate, to embrace long hugs, gently cup his face, kiss him tenderly, or try new things in the bedroom. He knew this about me when he married me, and now he wanted me to change.

After a major blowout that led to a week of silence, I sat on the couch at 2 a.m. for what felt like an eternity. Eventually, I gathered the courage to ask myself a crucial question: "What part do I have in all this?"

I wanted to place all the blame on him, but both partners are 100% responsible for the health of the marriage, and I didn't want a divorce. So, I recommitted and returned to my life coaching sessions to figure out why I was resisting and holding back the love my husband needed and deserved.

Let's be real—I was doing it unintentionally, but I knew it. It felt awkward and unfulfilled, leaving me to wonder if the emotions I thought I was expressing were even real. There was still so much to uncover, gain insights from, mend past wounds, and reprogram the messages and beliefs in my mind.

Revisiting My Coach

Working with my life coach, I realized my beliefs were outdated and harmful to both my relationship and personal growth. So, what if my husband wanted sex? It's a beautiful part of marriage, and I needed to confront my fears and redefine intimacy—not as a weakness, but as a strength that could deepen our connection and mend our rifts.

I wanted to be that flirty, sultry wife—the one who made him feel like the luckiest guy in the room, captivated by my newfound confidence. I desired him just as much as he desired me.

The challenge was being vulnerable enough to show it. This journey wasn't just about changing my behavior; it was about reshaping my mindset toward love, sex, intimacy, and vulnerability. I had to embrace discomfort and lean into moments that scared me, as they held the key to unlocking a deeper connection with my husband.

I discovered that fulfilling his fantasies and providing the emotional support he had sought all his life would also give me the husband I had always needed. As my life coach put it, "We were divinely orchestrated for one another."

Marriage is challenging, and filled with unique experiences, trauma, and pain. Yet, embracing these challenges together can transform a relationship into something extraordinary. Nothing spices up a marriage like tackling issues head-on and emerging stronger and sexier on the other side.

In this space of vulnerability and openness, I found the courage to communicate authentically with my husband, nurturing a marriage that combined the spicy passion of a perfectly seasoned dish with deep-rooted trust and understanding.

The Power of Vulnerability

Present day, the marriage I have is the one I dreamed of as far back as I can remember—full of passion, deep connection, and the love that makes my heart race and my skin tingle. It's a wild, beautiful ride where we still steal glances like we're each other's best-kept secret, and the playful touches feel like we're falling in love all over again.

If there's one thing I'd like you to reflect on, it's this: Embrace the journey of self-discovery and growth. This journey not only transforms you but also enriches the relationships you cherish, turning them into havens of love, understanding, and limitless possibilities

Often, reasons like fatigue, lack of time, age, work, or minor irritations may hinder your desire to invest in your marriage or intimacy. These reasons might serve as a protective shield, hiding deeper pain that prevents you from being vulnerable, open, and genuinely happy with your spouse.

However, when you uncover the true reasons, push past these barriers, and embrace vulnerability, you unlock the potential for a deeper connection that can reignite the passion and intimacy in your relationship—like adding a dash of fiery salsa to a classic dish, transforming it from bland to sizzling, and making every moment together a tantalizing dance of desire that leaves you both craving more.

About Becky Parker

Becky Parker is a passionate and dedicated Mindset Coach at Relationship Success 4 Life, on a mission to help women break free from the cycles of stress, overwhelm, and self-doubt that hold them back. Drawing deeply from her own journey and understanding of the daily struggles women face, Becky specializes in empowering her clients to rise above challenges, rebuild confidence, and embrace fulfilling, intimate relationships.**

Through transformative virtual coaching sessions, Becky offers a safe, supportive space for women to rediscover themselves, lean into their strengths, and redefine their lives with renewed clarity and purpose. Her approach is both compassionate and strategic, blending mindset mastery with actionable tools to help clients effortlessly juggle the demands of personal and professional life.

Becky's unwavering commitment to personal growth has touched and transformed the lives of countless women, empowering them to show up as their most authentic selves, feeling confident, beautiful, and in love—with both life and themselves. For women ready to invest in their future, find balance, and reclaim joy, Becky Parker is not just a coach but a partner in their journey to lasting happiness, connection, and success.

Get Becky's gift: www.InnerRevolutionBook.com/gift/Becky

Embrace the journey of self-discovery and growth.

Inner Revolution: Embracing Change to Achieve Greatness

When Sinking Is Not an Option
Dr. Sharon Ostermeir

Are you navigating the profound journey of widowhood, whether recently or for some time now? The path after losing a cherished spouse is undoubtedly filled with a tapestry of emotions, questions, and challenges. I have walked this path, and my heart is dedicated to uplifting fellow widows and widowers, helping them transform their lives. May my story serve as a beacon of hope and inspiration for you.

The Day Everything Changed

In less than 24 short hours, my life changed forever. My 56-year-old husband, business partner, and father of my three college-aged kids died suddenly. Losing my husband of 30 years, the most important person in my life, affected everything. I learned that the death of a spouse differs greatly from other losses and traumas, in that it changed every single aspect of my life.

The way I ate, slept, watched TV, worked, and lived was now different. My social circle and financial situation were different, too. It affected how I felt about myself, my confidence, self-esteem, health, interests, sense of security, and my sense of femininity. Everything changed.

The weeks following John's death were exceptionally hectic, busy, fast-paced, and a bit of a blur. My kids asked me if they could go back to college. They asked me if we had to move from the home we loved. Exceedingly difficult, valid questions. Honestly, I did not know.

Since I hadn't managed the family finances, my understanding of our financial situation was limited—a huge mistake I sadly came to regret. I explained to my kids that their job was to go back and do well in school, while mine was to work as hard as possible to keep us in our home for the time being. We had a choice: sink or swim, and sinking wasn't an option.

What I soon came to understand was quite a shock. My financial health was in shambles. There was no life insurance policy in place. The credit card debt was overwhelming, and the tax debt was even more substantial. Savings were non-existent. I had to borrow money just to cover the funeral expenses.

Hundreds of friends, family, and patients attended the wake and funeral. I knew I needed to take action. My husband and I co-owned a chiropractic practice. One week after his passing, I realized I had to return to my patients and rebuild the business to maintain my home, keep my kids in college, and pay off approximately $200,000 in debt.

Finding Support in Community

My practice and patients were my lifeline, keeping me occupied and grounded. My family—brother, sister, and parents—provided immense support, as did the friends my husband and I shared. Additionally, my staff and business coaches were incredibly helpful and understanding. My in-laws, also grieving, surprisingly kept their distance, which broke my heart for my children.

I attended an amazing eight-week bereavement group for young widows and widowers. However, at the end of a long workday, I returned home to a dark, empty, silent house. There was no one to greet me or inquire about my day. I ate alone, emptied the dishwasher alone, slept alone, went through the mail, and took out the garbage by myself. I didn't want to go out and socialize.

It felt as though my identity had changed. Who was I now? I was no longer a "we." I was now a "me." Turning that "w" to an "m" meant turning everything upside down. That's how I felt as a recent widow.

One afternoon, after enduring a long and challenging day, I found myself drawn to my local beach boardwalk to watch the sun go down and take a walk. The sunset was nothing short of magnificent, painting the sky with vibrant, awe-inspiring colors. As I walked, I experienced an "AH-HA" moment. In that instant, clarity washed over me, revealing my true path. I understood what I needed to focus on and where my heart wanted to lead me.

I realized I desired to reshape my life—to be present for my children, to embrace good health, to achieve financial stability, to foster strong social bonds, to facilitate healing, and to live a life filled with beauty and purpose. At that moment, I knew it was time to define my goals and map out the steps to bring them to fruition.

During that transformative period, my coaches were a tremendous support in setting my goals. I discovered that significant life events, whether joyous or challenging, serve as powerful catalysts for personal growth and change. The death of my spouse and the challenges I faced were definitely just that. I committed myself to creating a new, beautiful, abundant life. I came to understand that the first step on this remarkable adventure was to cultivate a positive mindset, setting the stage for boundless possibilities. I gave myself the space to grieve while embracing the opportunity to grow.

As a recent widow facing obstacles in every area of life, cultivating a positive mindset was challenging. I often pondered where to start. While maintaining a positive attitude at work, especially when caring for patients, came naturally, I realized I needed to extend that mindset to my personal life. To achieve this, I began reading books, exploring the internet, and listening to podcasts to transform my previously slightly negative outlook into a positive growth one.

Every morning, I begin my day by listing five things I'm grateful for in my journal. This simple yet powerful habit quickly transformed my mindset, helping me focus on reasons to be happy instead of dwelling on negatives. I appreciated sunny mornings, moments when my kids took out the trash, a smile from a stranger, and productive days at work. My gratitude also extended to holidays spent with family, unexpected calls from friends, or even the ability to pay my credit card bill. On some days, I was simply thankful for the ability to get out of bed.

Over time, I started incorporating gratitude and mindfulness into various aspects of my life. I made a habit of thanking and complimenting people throughout the day, genuinely expressing my appreciation. To keep gratitude at the forefront of my mind, I placed reminders around my home and office. I also rediscovered self-care, treating myself occasionally to lunch with a friend or a manicure. Reflecting on the golden rule, I aimed to treat others as I wished to be treated. Through this journey, I learned to appreciate, recognize, and value the positive elements in my life and the people around me.

The more I embraced gratitude, the more inspired I became to transform other essential aspects of my life.

Setting Goals for a New Life

The pivotal question I faced was: where do I begin on this journey toward a new "me" life, after years of living a "we" life? Following this enormous loss, my life felt like a blank canvas, urging me to reevaluate and redefine my identity.

I was lucky to get advice that helped me see my life as different parts, which I split it into six main areas: family and relationships, personal growth, health, spirituality, career, and money. In each area, I wrote three important goals in my journal. These goals gave me a new purpose and clarity about what steps I needed to take going forward.

My journey of transformation began with three foundational action steps in each area of my life. As I advanced, these steps naturally evolved, giving way to the next set of three, and so forth. Additional steps continued to emerge, each vital to my personal growth. Navigating the haze of "widow's fog" often made reality feel dreamlike or nightmarish, but I persevered. Each morning, I committed to waking up and writing down my gratitude. Alongside this practice, I diligently reviewed my action steps, ensuring steady progress toward my goals.

First, I needed to take charge of my financial future. Reducing debt, managing my finances efficiently, increasing my income, and curbing expenses were vital objectives. To reach these goals, I realized the importance of innovating within my business and expanding my career horizons. Creative thinking to establish additional income streams was essential. I had many tasks to tackle, like processing documents, reviewing and acquiring insurance policies, contacting social security, and scrutinizing bills. It also became apparent that I couldn't navigate this path by myself, making professional financial advice indispensable.

While financial management was essential, I soon realized that the other facets of my life required my attention. My health emerged as a top priority, especially since I aspired to be present for my children as they transitioned into adulthood. With this in mind, I took decisive action by hiring a transformational personal trainer. I mastered the art of weightlifting, gained insights into the significance of macros, and discovered the motivation to adopt a healthier lifestyle. As a chiropractor, I got adjusted regularly to keep my nervous system working optimally.

Another impactful change was integrating a daily routine of walking 10,000 steps, often at sunrise. This habit not only bolstered my physical health and led to weight loss but also provided a boost to my mental well-being. Walking at sunrise became a spiritual experience for me—the perfect way to embrace the start of a new day. Additionally, I explored other spiritual connections through practices like meditation, sound bath healing, reiki, and massage, all of which deepened my journey toward healing and wellness. These lifestyle changes one by one became daily routines.

Building Connections and Healing

Adjusting to life after losing a spouse is an overwhelming challenge that only those who have experienced it can truly understand. As a recent widow, I struggled to engage in anything beyond work, lacking motivation to socialize, and feeling the heavy weight of loneliness, even though I didn't want to go out. I now realize that these feelings were a natural part of my grieving process.

I was urged to join a local group for young widows and widowers. It began with a bereavement program and blossomed into meaningful social connections, friendships, and engaging activities. Joining this group was undoubtedly one of the best decisions I made for my healing process.

I was making significant progress with the action steps I had taken to achieve my goals. However, I still grappled with a deep sense of ache and sadness. I was introduced to a holistic trauma and recovery coach and began working with him. His holistic methods helped me to release the trauma that had been trapped within me. As I released the trauma, every other area of my life began to thrive, and I noticed many positive life-changing things happen.

Living a Life of Abundance

Today, I embrace a life overflowing with love, beauty, and abundance. My business is not just thriving; it's expanding beyond my dreams. I live in a lovely new home, unburdened by debt, and I'm enjoying the best health I've experienced in years. My three children are not only happy and successful but also kind-hearted individuals. We share a close, supportive bond with my mom, brother, sister, and their families. I have a wonderful circle of close friends. I'm blessed with a loving relationship, and my heart is full.

My grief didn't disappear. It changed. Often, it came and went like the tide—and sometimes it still does. The journey was not always easy. I never "got over" losing my husband John, but I've learned to carry that loss within me, using it as a driving source of healing and renewal. While I am whole once more, I acknowledge I am forever changed—and I wouldn't have it any other way. I take pride in the strength that I've discovered, what I have overcome, and the achievements I've reached on this journey.

About Dr. Sharon Ostermeir

Dr. Sharon Ostermeir is a Holistic Chiropractor with over 38 years of experience as the owner of Commack Chiropractic Care. She graduated cum laude with a Bachelor of Science degree in Biology from the University of Bridgeport and earned her Doctor of Chiropractic degree from New York Chiropractic College.

As a Board-eligible Neurology Diplomate, she holds certifications in Pediatrics, Women's Health, and Nutrition, emphasizing a holistic approach to care. Her practice focuses on structural, nutritional, and emotional balance, encouraging lifestyle changes for optimal health.

After the passing of her husband, Dr. Sharon embarked on a journey of rebuilding her life, which inspired her to help others, especially widows, transform their lives. To enhance her support for clients and patients, she became a certified Life and Success Coach, offering personalized one-on-one and group coaching sessions to foster growth and success.

Get a free gift from Dr. Sharon by visiting:

www.InnerRevolutionBook.com/gift/Sharon

Adjusting to life after losing a spouse is an overwhelming challenge that only those who have experienced it can truly understand.

Inner Revolution: Embracing Change to Achieve Greatness

Inner Revolution: Embracing Change to Achieve Greatness

From Anxiety to Adventure
Isabella Godinez, TNLP, TTT, THt, TSC, TEFT

It all started one afternoon when I got my graded final for Biology—a C! After hours of studying, skipping lunches, and staying after school, this grade felt like a slap in the face. Frustrated, I went to my mom that evening and said, "This grade doesn't reflect the effort I put in." At that moment, I realized the problem wasn't my lack of studying; it was the anxiety that took over on test day, wiping away everything I had learned.

Shifting My Mindset

I eventually realized that I could always choose a different approach and that my problems didn't define me. Previously, I felt powerless, reacting to circumstances, making no changes. After my finals, I knew I needed to shift my mindset. This is what Neuro-Linguistic Programming (NLP) refers to as moving from Effect to Cause. By taking charge of my situation, I could change the outcome or learn from my experiences. To help me navigate this process, I hired a life coach to identify the baggage I needed to let go of and understand why I hadn't thrown it out yet.

In the 4th grade, I realized my teacher had belittled me. After forgetting my backpack just ONCE, she called me out in front of the entire class. Another time, while walking with a friend to retrieve her lunch card, I ended up getting in trouble, resulting in a recess detention for simply being there with her.

These experiences made me aware of how authority figures treat younger students, especially those they don't like, or think are "dumb." This realization helped me understand the root of my testing anxiety, which contributed to my failing the biology final.

To address my anxiety, I worked with my coach and discovered T.I.M.E techniques. This approach allows you to explore past events that affect you, even if you can't pinpoint the exact moment. It's a valuable tool for anyone who experiences overwhelming emotions.

Now, I'm proud to say I completed a 4-6 hour written test, passed with flying colors, and felt comfortable asking the teacher questions. After my coach helped me through that difficult time, I knew I was ready to tackle many more challenges, just as you can!

I struggled with confidence issues. Whenever I bought something, I'd think, "It'll look cute when I lose a little weight or work out more." I chose clothes I thought were cute but never wore them because they made me uncomfortable.

My coach helped me focus on my self-confidence. She encouraged me to feel comfortable in my skin before expecting others to see that comfort. So, I challenge you: if you lack self-confidence or want to boost the confidence you already have, find one item in your closet that you love but haven't worn. You bought it for a reason! Whether you choose to wear it at home or out, step out of your comfort zone. Here's the kicker: if you feel good after doing it, keep going!

Reflecting on Education

April 2020—spring break, baby! Sike, it's COVID! We were told to go home with no idea of when we could come back out. That was my senior year of high school. I feel fortunate to have attended prom the year before because the Class of 2020 didn't get that chance. Through all the work I've done on myself, I can now look back with appreciation rather than resentment for what I missed.

Here's another "Do-It-With-Me" (DIWM) exercise: think of a time when you were angry at someone or yourself. Got it? Now, reflect on that moment. What can you find to be grateful for, or what lesson can you learn from it, now that you're looking from a different perspective? Notice how your feelings change when you shift your viewpoint.

There's a quote I hear often during training: "When you change the way you look at things, the things you look at change." It's not my quote, but I love it! This lesson came to me slowly but surely, and I believe you can learn it too. Recognizing different perspectives and understanding others' views of the world can deepen your compassion. Everyone sees the world differently, and respecting those perspectives enriches your own understanding.

With COVID rising, everyone had to adjust. We were thrown into online school, and I can honestly say I STRUGGLED. Juggling different computer courses, learning a new format for finding homework, figuring out how to listen to lectures, and wondering where to access my textbook—every day felt like a mental breakdown as I tried to adapt to this "new way" of schooling.

I also thought about how teachers and schools had to switch to online learning on such short notice. They had to upload or send everything with little time to prepare. Understanding their challenges kept me from getting upset or frustrated with them.

I switched to Southern New Hampshire University (SNHU) because they had more experience with online classes. This allowed me to explore different subjects and discover what I liked best. Like many students who planned to focus on a specific goal for the next two years, I wanted to be sure about my path, but uncertainty made me uneasy. I often wondered how many other second-year college students were still unsure about their major.

After earning my associate's degree, I took a break from college. I thought learning about neurons and the brain would be exciting, but it wasn't. What truly resonated with me were the insights from my coach while she taught me new skills. Her positive attitude and genuine desire to help others stood out, and that was something I could be interested in!

Recognizing My Strengths and Dreams

People often told me, "You're so mature for your age," or "You're great at giving advice." At first, I didn't get why this mattered. I was good at giving "boy advice," even though I had never been in a relationship. It was strange to have ideas about something I hadn't gone through myself. But somehow, my thoughts still helped others.

That's when I saw it—the opportunity that could change my life. My coach shared her experience with a course that transformed her into the amazing person and businesswoman she is today. It was called Create Your Life, a three-day workshop focused on self-discovery and envisioning the person you want to become. Excited about my future, my mom and I signed up together. By the end of the workshop, she had learned a lot about herself and even sought a coach to help her with some old issues. I realized that my passion lies in helping others learn and become their best selves—that's what I want to do!

However, as the course ended, I felt I wasn't finished. Doubts crept in about pursuing something so "different." Not attending college for the full four years like most of my family felt strange. Questions flooded my mind: "Would they judge me?" The uncertainty about my future weighed heavily on me as I worried about whether others would support or believe in me.

This was a monumental moment—my big chance. While some people take a year off to travel or work instead of immediately going to college, I wondered if my chosen path would be accepted. Understanding the importance of education, I sought a path that would help my future career, even if it wasn't psychology. This led me to join a program to become a Hypnotherapist, Coach, and NLP Practitioner.

Signing up for the *Create Your Life* workshop has empowered me to believe in and create the life I want. Who would've thought! I was excited to continue my education in a way that made me happy. One thing I knew for sure was that I wanted to travel. That's it—just travel. I hadn't thought about any specifics, which was a problem in how I approached this goal.

While studying, I also had coaching calls where I expressed my desire to travel. My coach urged me to be more specific. "Okay, pause, Linda," I said (As a joke, I call everyone Linda in the nicest way possible, not like a Karen). I realized I hadn't thought it through! My coach gave me a look that said, "Oh, Linda, you're about to discover exactly what, where, how, and when all of this will happen."

She used a tactic to help me create achievable outcomes by using SMART Goals. We set a specific date for my goal and wrote what I would have, do, or be as part of it, along with the sights, sounds, and feelings associated with it. By including all these details and the personal qualities that would help me achieve my goal, it felt like a future event that had already happened. I could see it happening as I had written it.

I asked myself important questions that helped clarify my goal. It seemed so possible and real that I felt like I couldn't fail! The next day, I was focused and motivated, determined to find a van to convert into a travel vehicle for exploring the United States this summer and fall. It was amazing! I wondered where all this energy came from as I typed on Facebook Marketplace to find a van.

Achieving My Van Life Dream

Less than three months later, after checking out two vans, I drove home with the second one. It felt incredible to have my van and get it ready for my first adventure! But the journey didn't stop there. After a trip to the mechanic, I learned I needed new shocks, tire rods, control arms, and a few other repairs. YAY ME! No seriously, though—YAY me for having a van to travel and live in all around the world. Perspective baby!

Getting ready to leave took a few months. It felt like the right time for a change. Sometimes friends aren't available when you need them, and many people hesitate to do exciting things because they fear going alone or trying something new. While sitting around the fire with friends one night, I looked up from the fire and noticed they were all somewhere else. I was sitting at the fire alone.

In that moment, I asked myself, "If I were out here by myself right now, would I feel comfortable? Would I have music playing? Would I have built a fire or ventured into the dark?" Recognizing that I wasn't entirely comfortable prompted me to reflect on how I could learn to enjoy nature's beauty by myself. This was my experiment with expanding my comfort zone.

How does our comfort zone grow? By doing things that make us <u>uncomfortable</u>. It's impossible to feel more at ease with new experiences without being willing to face some discomfort first. This realization helped me decide to plan a solo trip—to take the van out and take care of myself, the van, and my dog.

While scrolling Instagram, I found a van event in the desert featuring a variety of rigs. It felt crazy, but I signed up for an email to learn more about it and began planning my trip. There was uncertainty about whether I'd ever feel ready, but I intentionally stepped outside my comfort zone. I'm someone who thrives on routine, so I usually plan and prepare extensively. However, I couldn't over-prepare for this experience, which is why I reserved my spot months in advance.

If you find it hard to start something new, just pick a date you have to stick to because "the right time" never really comes. So, there I was, starting my first solo trip—scared but feeling free.

The drive was incredible; it was my first time on the road! As I traveled, it rained. I knew I had to overcome this challenge alone. There was no option to switch seats or ask someone else to drive—I had to get comfortable immediately. Sitting just two inches from the wheel, with sweaty palms, panting breath, and a shaking foot pressing the gas, I felt the urgency. All I could think was, "Don't hydroplane, don't crash, don't roll backward."

Worrying made it worse, so I scanned my mind for any technique I could use. I remembered a technique for releasing anxiety: instead of focusing on what might go wrong, I visualized myself calmly acting—turning on my blinker, switching lanes, slowly making turns. I focused on the outcome I wanted, and gradually, I calmed down. If you're afraid of driving in the rain or snow, try this approach. Afterward, you'll have added a new experience to your comfort zone. What will you add next?

After a tense ten-minute drive, I finally found the nomad community I had been longing for since buying my van—other nomads and potential friends along my journey. I parked among a group of vans, sat inside, and told myself, "You have two choices: go out there shy and miss the chance to make friends, OR you go out there knowing you're a boss, and make it everything you want!"

About Isabella Godinez

Isabella Godinez is a dedicated Trainer of Neuro-Linguistic Programming, Clinical Hypnotherapy, and Coaching, with two years of professional experience and many more years as a client herself. She graduated from Transform Destiny, earning board certifications in NLP, Hypnotherapy, Coaching, EFT, and TIME Techniques.

Isabella specializes in helping students navigate transitional phases, such as switching or graduating schools, and improving communication between parents and children. She chose these specialties because she overcame these same life challenges. She supports anxious students and employees, young adults seeking career direction, and individuals working to enhance their confidence and self-worth.

As the creator of "NLP With Me," Isabella focuses on making transitions smooth and enjoyable, empowering her clients to communicate effectively, accomplish their goals with confidence, and envision their desired futures. Her compassionate approach fosters self-esteem, helping individuals feel positively about their actions, beliefs, and identities.

To receive Isabella's gift, visit:

www.InnerRevolutionBook.com/gift/Isabella

It's impossible to feel more at ease with new experiences without being willing to face some discomfort first.

Inner Revolution: Embracing Change to Achieve Greatness

Embracing Resilience in the Midst of Unexpected Challenges and Changes

Shreve Gould, EMBA

Imagine a tree bending in a storm. The winds howl, and the rain lashes down, yet the tree stands tall despite the chaos, bending just enough to avoid breaking. You may strive for this image of resilience but find it difficult to embody it, especially in the face of unexpected challenges. Whether it's a sudden job loss, a health scare, or a natural disaster, life storms can leave you feeling overwhelmed and emotionally shaken. These events can make you feel stuck, stopped, stalled, or even lost and removed from your overall goals in life. But just like the tree, you can bend without breaking.

Resilience is more than suffering or surviving a hardship or a significant event. It's about bouncing back from and through adversity, adapting, and keeping moving, even when the road ahead is uncertain. Neuro-Linguistic Programming (NLP) offers powerful tools for cultivating this resilience. By exploring how your identity, Values, and Beliefs affect your ability to weather life's storms and by learning to reframe your experiences, remove negative emotions, eliminate limiting decisions, and release anchors to negative experiences, you can become more resilient in the face of life's inevitable challenges.

Inner Revolution: Embracing Change to Achieve Greatness

In this chapter, you'll discover how NLP can strengthen your emotional resilience, mental toughness, and adaptability, helping you navigate the unexpected with grace and strength.

Resilience and Its Foundations: Identity, Values, and Beliefs

Resilience isn't just about "toughing it out." It's about having the emotional agility to adapt when things don't go as planned. Your capacity for resilience is rooted in how you see yourself (your identity), what you value (your core values). and what you believe about the world (your beliefs),

Identity and Resilience

Your identity is the foundation of how you respond to the world. If you identify as someone who is "strong" or "capable," you're likely to approach challenges with a problem-solving mindset. Conversely, if your identity is tied to being a victim of circumstances, you might feel powerless when unexpected events occur.

For example, imagine you've just lost your job or are going through a divorce. If you see yourself as resourceful and adaptable, you will likely view this setback as an opportunity to explore alternative paths. However, if you identify as someone who always encounters bad luck, you may feel paralyzed by the loss, unsure how to move forward.

Through NLP techniques, you can shift your sense of identity to one that supports resilience. You can learn to see yourself as someone who can handle adversity, even when life throws curveballs. For instance, after losing my left leg, I don't identify as disabled; I see myself as forever adapting, which empowers me and widens my view of the world.

Question: *What Identify do you need to shift that will serve you better?*

Values and Resilience

Your core values—those things you hold most dear—shape your motivations and how you prioritize your responses to adversity. When your values align with your goals, you are better able to persevere through tough times.

If you value independence, losing your job may be distressing. But if you can shift your perspective to see how this loss can lead to greater independence (by starting your own business), your resilience will be strengthened. NLP helps you realign your values with your goals, allowing you to remain focused and adaptable in the face of unexpected change.

Beliefs and Resilience

Beliefs are the unconscious rules you hold about yourself and the world. Some beliefs support resilience ("I can handle anything that comes my way"), while others weaken it ("I'm not good enough to succeed"). These limiting beliefs often stem from experiences, particularly traumatic or stressful events.

Consider a professional who was let go from a job. If they internalize the belief that they are not good enough or capable, this belief may follow them into future endeavors, undermining their confidence and resilience when new challenges arise.

NLP can help by identifying and changing these limiting beliefs. Techniques such as belief re-imprinting or NLP Time Techniques allow you to replace unhelpful beliefs with ones that foster resilience. This might involve recognizing that one setback doesn't define your worth or understanding that failure is simply a stepping stone to growth.

Question: *What limiting beliefs about yourself, or others do you need to challenge and find a new belief to serve you better?*

Techniques to Strengthen Resilience

NLP offers practical tools for building emotional resilience, mental toughness, and adaptability. By using NLP techniques such as reframing, anchoring, NLP Time Techniques, and belief-change strategies, you can cultivate resilience in the face of life's challenges.

Reframing: Changing the Meaning of an Event

Reframing is a core NLP technique that involves changing the way you perceive an event or experience. By shifting the frame through which you view a situation, you can change your emotional response to it.

For instance, consider someone active who has experienced a significant health issue. Imagine facing a sudden loss, like losing a leg after a series of medical crises, like I did in August 2022. Others might say it's a tragedy. But using reframing techniques, you could discuss where the tragedy truly lies. If I hadn't had the operation to remove my left leg, I might not be alive. Is losing my leg to live really a tragedy?

I have shared with many that this is my next grand adventure, learning to live with a prosthetic leg. I experienced taking my first steps again as an adult. How cool is that? I have approached this experience through the lens of curiosity. I see this as an opportunity for personal growth or a chance to reassess what matters in my life. This shift in perspective has skyrocketed my resilience, allowing me to approach recovery with a more positive and empowered mindset. I was not always this resilient in my life. Along with my faith and purpose, it took learning NLP to become this resilient.

Scientific research supports the power of reframing. A study by Stipancic et al. (2010) found that individuals who underwent NLP-based reframing techniques reported higher levels of emotional resilience and reduced anxiety, demonstrating that reframing can improve mental adaptability during stressful times.

Reframing allows you to step back from your initial emotional reaction and view a situation from a broader perspective. When faced with a significant event, consider asking yourself questions like, "What else could this mean?" and "How can I learn and grow from this experience?" By thoughtfully answering these questions, you can transform adversity into a steppingstone instead of an obstacle.

Managing Emotional States

Anchoring is a powerful NLP technique that involves associating a particular emotional state with a physical trigger. For example, if you've ever felt a surge of confidence when listening to a favorite song, that song has become an "anchor" for confidence. By intentionally creating positive anchors, you can access empowering emotional states (such as calm, confidence, or focus) whenever you need them.

Anchoring is especially useful in high-stress situations. If you're about to give an important presentation and feel anxious, you can anchor the feeling of calm to a simple physical gesture (like pressing your thumb and index finger together), triggering a calm state when anxiety rises.

On the flip side, removing programmed anchors can help you break free from negative emotional states tied to certain experiences. If a specific environment or event triggers feelings of fear or insecurity, NLP techniques can help remove those negative responses, replacing them with more helpful emotions.

Tosey and Mathison (2003) found that individuals trained in NLP techniques like anchoring showed greater resilience in high-pressure environments. By anchoring positive emotions and removing negative ones, you can approach challenges with a greater sense of calm and focus.

Removing Negative Emotions and Limiting Beliefs

NLP Time Techniques provide a powerful way to release negative emotions and limiting beliefs tied to past events. These techniques allow you to "travel" back along your internal timeline to the root of an emotional issue, negative belief, or limiting decision, and then remove its emotional impact.

For example, if you feel a deep sense of fear every time you face uncertainty, this fear may stem from a specific past event, like an earlier failure. You can revisit that event in your mind using NLP Time Techniques, releasing the negative emotion attached to it. This process frees you from the emotional weight of the past, enabling you to face new challenges with greater resilience and clarity.

Similarly, limiting beliefs such as "I'm not capable" or "I always fail" often form from past decisions made in moments of distress. NLP Time Techniques allow you to return to when those limiting decisions were made, re-examine them from a new perspective, and let go of them. Once you release those beliefs, you can replace them with more empowering ones supporting your ability to adapt and grow in adversity.

Wake et al. (2013) explored the impact of NLP on recovering from significant emotional events, demonstrating that techniques like NLP Time Techniques can help you remove emotional anchors linked to negative experiences. By doing so, you'll experience increased emotional resilience.

NLP's Impact on Resilience

Let's explore scientific studies and real-life examples of unexpected changes and challenges of how NLP enhances resilience.

Study 1: NLP and Emotional Resilience

In a study by Stipancic et al. (2010), participants who underwent NLP interventions reported significant improvements in emotional resilience. Techniques such as reframing, belief-change, and NLP Time Techniques helped individuals reduce anxiety and develop a more positive outlook on challenges. The study showed that NLP can improve emotional adaptability, particularly during stressful and uncertain times.

Consider a real-life example of a professional who lost their job and initially saw the experience as a failure, which triggered feelings of anxiety and helplessness. However, by using NLP reframing techniques, they could shift their perspective, viewing the job loss as a chance to explore their passions and create a more fulfilling career. This change in mindset empowered them to take proactive steps, leading to a more rewarding professional journey.

Study 2: NLP for Cognitive and Behavioral Flexibility

Research by Tosey and Mathison (2003) found that NLP techniques like anchoring increased cognitive and behavioral flexibility. Participants who learned to anchor positive emotional states could maintain focus and calm under pressure, improving their mental toughness in high-stakes environments.

A real-life example of using NLP for cognitive and behavioral flexibility involves a mother struggling to move past the emotions of a natural disaster she had experienced. Her fear of uncertainty kept resurfacing, affecting her ability to cope with new challenges. By applying NLP Time Techniques, she could revisit the root of her fear, release the negative emotions associated with it, and shift her perspective. This process significantly improved her emotional resilience, enabling her to face future challenges with greater calm, focus, and mental toughness, free from the emotional weight of her experiences.

Practical Application: How to Build Resilience with NLP

You can cultivate resilience through NLP, empowering yourself to face life's challenges with strength and adaptability. Here's how you can begin:

1. Explore Your Identity: Reflect on how you see yourself. Do you identify as resilient, adaptable, and capable? If not, consider how you can shift your identity to support a more empowering narrative.

2. Align Your Values: Assess your core values and ensure they align with your goals. Re-evaluate your values and how they guide your responses to adversity.

3. Identify Limiting Beliefs: Explore your beliefs about yourself and the world. Are there any limiting beliefs holding you back? Use NLP techniques to reframe these beliefs and replace them with ones that empower you.

4. Practice Reframing: When facing challenges, consciously practice reframing the situation. Ask yourself, "What else could this mean?" or "How can I learn from this experience?"

5. Use Anchoring: Identify and create positive emotional anchors. Practice using them in stressful situations to enhance your emotional resilience.

6. Engage with NLP Time Techniques: Learn and practice NLP Time Techniques to release negative emotions and limiting beliefs from experiences. This process will free you from emotional weight and increase your ability to adapt to new challenges.

Resilience as a Journey

Resilience is not a fixed trait, but a skill you can nurture through practice and self-awareness. With the tools offered by NLP, you can shift your identity, beliefs, and values to strengthen your emotional resilience, mental toughness, and adaptability. Techniques like reframing, creating positive anchors, removing negative emotions through NLP Time Techniques, and challenging limiting beliefs empower you to face life's challenges with confidence and grace. To be resilient, one needs to learn to look through the lens of curiosity; what can I learn about myself and others in this experience? We become more resilient when we embrace an identity of resilience, supported by corresponding values, beliefs, and behaviors. We are now able to embrace resilience in the midst of unexpected challenges and changes

Remember, resilience isn't about never bending—it's about bending without breaking. Like the tree in the storm, you have the power to remain grounded and emerge stronger. Life's challenges may shake you, and with the right mindset and tools, you can remain grounded, adaptable, and strong, no matter what comes your way. Deep Roots, Strong Branches.

About Shreve Gould

Shreve Gould is a Master NLP Practitioner and Master Success Coach known for his unique ability to blend intellectual depth with emotional insight. With an Executive MBA from Emory University's Goizueta Business School, Shreve brings a strategic and human-centered approach to fostering resilience and growth. His distinguished military career as a Major in the U.S. Army, including a deployment in 2009 where he received the Bronze Star (M) for his actions, instilled in him a profound understanding of leadership under pressure.

In August 2022, after losing his left leg, Shreve's resilience was once again tested, and he emerged stronger, continuing to inspire and guide others through personal and professional challenges. His exceptional ability to connect logical analysis with empathy allows him to create impactful coaching experiences that empower individuals and organizations to adapt and thrive.

To receive Shreve's gift, visit:

www.InnerRevolutionBook.com/gift/Shreve

Remember, resilience isn't about never bending—it's about bending without breaking.

Living My Vision Board Life

Jo Ann Long, TNLP, TTT, TCHt

It was a cool evening in November 2002. The top floor of the building was decorated with Christmas lights and glitter. The band played softly as the singles group gathered. Over my right shoulder stood a tall, handsome man in a suit with faint stripes. His tie was yellow with diamond shapes.

A staff member read our names from our badges. Jo Ann, McKinney. Craig, Flower Mound. We shook hands and started what turned out to be the most amazing experience I ever had.

Craig acted like he didn't know where McKinney was. He didn't know that I grew up there and was a true Texas Farm Girl. He told me he was from California. I quickly replied, "I'm going to live there one day!" He smiled big and asked, "Where?" I said, "La Jolla." He then asked, "Can I wave at you when I sail by in my sailboat?" I said, "Sure!"

As we talked more, we found out we like many of the same hobbies. We both enjoy horseback riding, golfing, scuba diving, boating, taking cruises, parasailing, zip lining, and snow skiing.

During our talk, we both agreed that believing in something bigger and being spiritual were especially important to us. Knowing this made me feel good about myself and made it easy to share my feelings.

Inner Revolution: Embracing Change to Achieve Greatness

The Power of Personal Transformation

That wasn't always the case in my life. I grew up with low self-esteem and a fear of expressing my feelings and beliefs due to the risk of criticism. This made it difficult for me to trust myself, especially after making decisions that had negative outcomes, and it also fueled my fear of trusting others, as I had been deeply hurt in the past.

When I met Craig, I had been a single mom for twelve years. In a counseling session, I learned that if I didn't change, I would probably choose another partner just like before. I was determined not to let that happen. So, I started improving myself.

I read books and watched Dr. Phil McGraw. In the 1980s, I recorded his show on 8-track tape and watched it in the evenings. I cut out newspaper articles and drove sixty miles to a weekly group counseling session for nine months, even in bad weather. And I prayed.

Words are important. How you say things and what you think about yourself matters, so I really needed to stop thinking bad things about myself. Then, I met Dr. Ray Walker, a pastor, and a Doctor of Divinity. He had a course on Graphology, which is the study of handwriting.

When he analyzed my handwriting, he revealed the fears I harbored and the defense mechanisms I had developed to navigate my life—both the one I was born into and the one I was currently living in. I was shocked by his insights. It felt as if he had taken my blood and provided a report on my physical health, but instead, he was uncovering the issues in my subconscious mind. I realized I was in a very troubled state!

I learned you could change your handwriting, and it would change the subconscious mind, but if you listened to hypnosis recordings of guided meditations, the subconscious mind would change, and it would be faster and easier. So, he asked me what in my analysis I wanted to change, and he recorded those suggestions for me. I changed, as did my handwriting. And my life and world changed all for the better.

Discovering Vision Boards

A friend I met through Dr. Walker invited me to her church in Dallas, where I discovered my first book on vision boards. Although I had heard about vision boards before, this book felt like exactly what I needed. I was so eager to absorb the information that I could hardly put it down. Every page inspired me and even showed me step-by-step how to create my own.

Magazines became a staple; I purchased many, visited the library for their old issues, and with permission brought home copies from office visits. I even collected magazines from travel agencies and tourist offices.

The instructions were simple: dream about the life I wanted. I was encouraged to imagine the places I wanted to visit, the car I wanted to drive, the house, furniture, and even the person I wanted to become. I had to consider my ideal lifestyle—hobbies, clothes, jewelry, and even food. The book also advised including ways to make money, since the Law of Attraction says you get what you ask for, but you still need money to avoid debt.

When choosing what to put on the board, I didn't focus on how it would come true. Instead, I just picked what caught my eye, even though most of it didn't reflect my current life. I added pictures of a woman golfing, a small house in the snow, a small boat harbor, a cruise ship, a small airplane, and a California beach. Then, I wrote "A California Lifestyle" and included images of a horse, a stereo, a hand-drawn book cover, a pretend business check, a lottery check, food, jewelry, clothes, an American Airlines plane, a European cruise, the Eiffel Tower, The Louvre, France, Greece, Italy, the Caribbean, a backyard hot tub, and more.

I glued the pictures onto construction paper and hung them on the wall of my rented house. Sometimes, I would stand and just look at them, then add more. One day, I noticed a picture of a stereo on the board and realized I had recently bought one. I ran downstairs and was amazed to see that the real stereo was exactly like the one in the picture.

That was the moment I thought, "Wow! This really works."

Building My Vision Board Life

From that moment on, I believed I could live the life of my dreams. I knew I could create it with God's help. I realized I needed to plan my life carefully because my dreams could come true.

Important things happened quickly, like learning to play golf and purchasing my first house in a golf course neighborhood. Earning both beginners and advanced scuba diving certifications led to a memorable cruise to the Bahamas for diving. After skiing just once in high school, a trip to Colorado was a significant step up.

As I saw things on my board coming true, I kept improving myself. Whenever I tried something new, it took courage to step out of my comfort zone and face my fears. I kept growing, and so did my life, job, and friendships.

Recognizing the changes was difficult at first. I faced some truly challenging experiences that made me realize a better life lay beyond what I had known in my family. While I sensed there was more to life, the purpose and connections of everything remained unclear.

Carrying the pain and problems from the past persisted. After rereading that book, version 3.0 of my vision board took shape. Becoming a real estate agent prompted the search for pictures of desired properties, including apartment buildings, land, and a spec house building project. Thoughts turned to meeting a potential husband, prompting a list of traits that would complement my strong, independent nature. A husband who travels for work seemed like a good fit, along with a crucial requirement: no issues with alcohol.

I put a picture of a man in a suit holding a briefcase, someone with a professional job. I also had a picture of a man in blue jeans and a brown bomber jacket. This showed someone who cared about how he looked. I cut the heads off the pictures because I thought it was too much to include. The man in the picture was tall, dark, and handsome.

My life felt like I had been lost in a desert for a long time, waiting to reach a better place. This went on for years. My thoughts had grown, and my view of the world differed from how I was raised. I welcomed change instead of being afraid of it. I dreamed of a much better life. Before, I just reacted to things and had a poverty mentality. I was ready to find a suitable partner to share my life with and build something lasting. I had grown tremendously.

Manifesting My Soulmate

In the past, I would have been worried about meeting someone new. Is he the one? Is he right for me? This time, two weeks after the Christmas party where I met Craig, I opened the binder with my vision board and looked at the first page. When I made the 3.0 version, I added a timeline of when I wanted things to happen. "Meeting My Soulmate" was supposed to happen within a few months.

The next page had real estate investments, and one of those had already happened. One showed the "California Lifestyle," and Craig was from California. On the next page, a ski house appeared, and his family owns a ski condominium unit.

Another page had a picture of an American Airlines airplane, which meant I wanted to fly to vacation places like Europe. Craig is a Captain for American Airlines. He wore the same suit and tie. He talked about his pilot bomber jacket at the party. I knew for sure he was the one.

What an amazing life we've had! Here are some highlights: we bought a sailboat and lived on it in Southern California and Mexico, went scuba diving with Caribbean Reef Sharks, and purchased an airplane hangar that includes a home and a small plane. We also bought a house on a golf course, where we became members, and recently installed a spa.

Many cruises have taken us to incredible destinations, including The Louvre and The Eiffel Tower. Our travels have extended to Greece and Italy, and we even went on a safari in South Africa where we chased rhinos on foot. Zip lining is a favorite adventure along with helicopter tours. We run multiple businesses, including real estate.

Creating a Legacy

This serves as a testament that what you imagine can come true. As Craig and I built our life together, one of the most exciting aspects was blending our hobbies, interests, and dreams. We began exploring how to respect each other's values and goals while creating a life that balanced business and travel.

It was around this time, through a personal development community, that I met a couple who had built a seven-figure personal development company by producing life-changing courses. They had created systems and templates to follow, and their journey inspired us. After packing up all their belongings, they traveled the world for five years, embracing a nomadic lifestyle with the help of the latest technology. This opened our eyes to new possibilities.

Craig and I knew we still needed more personal development, so we hired him to be our coach. He taught us how to smooth out the rough edges and blind spots of ourselves, how to monetize our gifts and talents, and how to duplicate what he taught us to create a ripple effect with the powerful concepts of Neuro-Linguistic Programming.

Live Intentionally for Transformation

Since then, I founded the Center for L.I.F.T. ~ Live Intentionally for Transformation, with a mission to empower individuals to lead themselves, design a life of purpose with strategic intention, and build a legacy of wealth and impact. Through my signature course, Envision to Success, you will uncover your purpose, understand your core values, and discover what truly drives you. As you break free from feeling stuck, your fears and limiting beliefs—like "I can't do that," "I can't have that," or "I'm broke"—will dissolve.

You'll also experience growth in your relationships and learn how to shift your perspective, seeing life as something that happens for you, not to you. This course helps you set and achieve meaningful goals, and you can take part in a live vision board group to manifest your dreams.

Start today by creating your first vision board. Gather images that reflect your dreams, without worrying about how or when they'll come true. Include your "someday I'll do this" ambitions, along with ways to generate income.

Personal development requires both time and financial investment. Partner with someone like me who can guide you in getting the life, values, and integrity you desire—and help you build a community you want to be part of.

You've heard my story. Now, it's time to create yours. What are you waiting for?

About Jo Ann Long

Jo Ann Long, Founder and CEO of Center for L.I.F.T., LLC, is a dedicated professional with over five years of experience empowering women to achieve their entrepreneurial dreams. Specializing in women in the second half of life, Jo Ann guides her clients in creating sustainable businesses that can ensure a comfortable retirement while leaving a meaningful legacy.

Through her transformative approach, she helps clients release negative emotions and limiting beliefs, enabling them to discover their true purpose. By harnessing their unique gifts, Jo Ann supports them in monetizing their legacies with effective templates.

In addition to her coaching career, Jo Ann has significantly expanded her real estate portfolio, demonstrating her commitment to personal and professional growth. As a student pilot pursuing certification, she embodies an adventurous spirit, a love of travel, and has a mobile lifestyle. Jo Ann's dedication to lifelong learning drives her to explore the globe, making her a trusted mentor for women seeking to thrive in their entrepreneurial journeys.

Get a free gift from Jo Ann by visiting:

www.InnerRevolutionBook.com/gift/Jo-Ann

Gather images that reflect your dreams, without worrying about how or when they'll come true.

Transformation Through Loss
Rev. Donna Baranyay, CT, CCHt, CSC, B.Msc, MS

We experience loss, trauma, grief... an event occurs that changes the trajectory of our life plans. A loved one may die, a best friend moves away at a key moment in our life, a relationship ends that we thought might be forever, a job change, a geographical move that wasn't our choice, an illness, or injury that incapacitates us, and the list goes on.

Experiencing a loss of some kind changes us. It reshapes the contours of our existence, leaving imprints on our hearts and minds that are often both profound and indelible. Whether it is the loss of a loved one, a cherished dream, or a significant life opportunity, the impact of loss can ripple through every aspect of our lives. It can feel as though the ground beneath us has shifted, leaving us disoriented and unsure of how to move forward. Yet, within this disorientation lies the potential for remarkable transformation.

What happens when we experience a loss in our lives? Loss can be a catalyst for change. When we can shift our attitude towards loss, great things can unfold. This shift does not minimize the pain or invalidate the grief; rather, it allows us to see loss through a different lens. Instead of viewing it solely as an end, we can recognize it as a catalyst for growth and new beginnings. By embracing a mindset that acknowledges the lessons and opportunities hidden within our losses, we can uncover strengths and capacities we never knew we possessed.

> *"If you want something you've never had, you must be willing to do something you've never done."—Thomas Jefferson.*

One of the first steps in this transformation is to allow ourselves to fully experience and process our emotions. It is important to honor the grief, sadness, and even anger that loss can bring. These emotions are a natural response to change and should not be suppressed or ignored. By giving ourselves permission to feel, we create space for healing and for the eventual emergence of resilience.

Loss has a unique way of breaking us open, exposing the raw and vulnerable parts of ourselves that we often keep hidden. It forces us to confront our deepest fears and insecurities, challenging our perceptions of control and permanence. Amid this upheaval, we have a choice: to remain entrenched in our sorrow or to seek the hidden opportunities for growth, renewal, new strengths, insights, and possibilities within ourselves.

> *"The only way to make sense out of change is to plunge into it, move with it, and join the dance."—Alan Watts*

Shifting our attitude towards loss doesn't mean denying our pain or pretending that everything is okay. Rather, it involves a conscious decision to approach our grief with a sense of openness and curiosity. By embracing our emotions and allowing ourselves to fully experience them, we create space for healing and transformation.

As we navigate the journey of loss, we may find that our priorities and values shift. What once seemed important may no longer hold the same significance, and we may develop a deeper appreciation for the present moment and the people in our lives. This newfound perspective can inspire us to live more authentically and to pursue our passions with renewed vigor. Loss can teach us to live more fully, with greater compassion and empathy for ourselves and others.

"Change your thoughts and you change your world."— Norman Vincent Peale

By having the courage to change our thoughts, we can let go of what no longer serves us. When we do this, we find the courage to discover the Higher Truth of who we are. We are changing our outside world - or the experiences, events, and whatever else is a part of "our world." Its appearances are shifting because of the interior changes we are making from within.

I believe the crux of the grieving process is an internal shift. We are re-discovering ourselves. Some people may say that we are re-inventing ourselves.

Inevitability of Change

Even though we dislike change, change is inevitable. Change comes in many forms. Fear can keep us from embracing it. Fear of the unknown, moving out of our comfort zone, saying goodbye to someone we love, facing a sometimes-scary world alone—all can affect how we grieve.

Sometimes we face our fears with an outside support system and there are times we have to face parts of our journey alone. When we can tap into our inner resilience, we find the strength to keep going in the face of fear, uncertainty, and loss. We must learn to trust — trust ourselves and one another.

When we trust ourselves enough to allow ourselves to feel, we open the door to healing. When we begin the healing process, transformation can be a part of the result. I don't believe transformation is ever complete. We continue to be transformed with every experience, every opportunity for growth.

We can experience transformation at any time. It can be as the result of a death of a loved one, a midlife crisis, a shift in perspective, a spiritual awakening, a conscious choice to make a change or do something differently. It can be a quiet shift, an "aha" moment, or it can feel earth-shattering. We may choose to share it with a trusted loved one or we can keep it to ourselves. There is no end to the experience called transformation.

Goldilocks Experience

"If we don't change, we don't grow. If we don't grow, we aren't really living."—Gail Sheehy.

When I think of the healing process in grief, I think of what I call the Goldilocks' experience. We try different things until we discover what truly fits in our new journey. Just like the story *Goldilocks and the Three Bears*, we sometimes need to try new things until they feel right.

It can be an exhausting process and yet, can be incredibly healing at the same time. What I find important to remember is to give myself permission to let it take as long as needed. There's no specific timeline for healing; I heal at my pace and in my way. Healing from loss isn't "one-stop shopping" or a "one size fits all" reality.

It's so easy to slip into judging ourselves instead of being gentle with our self-talk. I try not to compare my experience with someone else's. One of my teachers, Rev. Juanita Gardner, taught me well. I still remember her sharing "try not to compare your insides to someone else's outsides" in one of our many conversations. This wisdom has been a guiding light, or inner compass, for me during my healing.

Our Inner Compass

"Simply touching a difficult memory with some slight willingness to heal begins to soften the holding and tension around it." - Stephen Levine

When I think of a compass, I think of a device that helps us find direction and stay on course when we are hiking or going on some kind of trip. I believe our inner compass could be defined as what grounds us, keeps us feeling safe in a perceived unsafe world. It can keep us anchored and grounded when we are feeling off kilter or losing our sense of direction, showing the pathway to healing.

Our compass can include facing a hard emotion, memory, or fear in order to begin the healing process. Some say that the journey of a thousand miles begins with one step (Lao Tzu). The journey towards healing and thriving starts the minute we make the choice to take that first step.

What is your compass? What does your compass look like?

Tools for Transformation and Achieving Greatness

What drew me to write this chapter was the power of the title. When I broke it down and explored the meanings of the words, it resonated deeply. "Inner" refers to "within" or "inside," while "revolution" means "a change" or "transformation." To me, this means we can transform from within—it's an "inside job."

What is it we want to change within ourselves to achieve greatness? It's important to remember that greatness is a personal concept. What I define as greatness may differ from others. For each of us, greatness is something meaningful on an individual level.

For some, greatness might mean earning a degree, starting a business, serving others, raising a family, or focusing on personal growth. There's no single definition—it's unique to each of us.

There are many tools to help us embrace change and achieve greatness. The first step is choosing a positive attitude and being willing to transform negative expectations into positive ones. I suggest going further and shifting from expectations to a mindset of expectancy. This approach opens us to receiving good with no need to define exactly how it will look.

For example, when we expect healing or positive change, we open ourselves to it without dictating the outcome. We often unknowingly expect things to look a certain way. It's important to acknowledge sadness, pain, and other feelings, but also set an intention to heal and move forward.

We can achieve greatness even as we navigate change. Embracing the new life ahead of us requires confidence and the willingness to invite joy and happiness. These experiences are deeply personal—how joy and happiness show up will be different for each of us, but both our inner world and outer life will reflect them.

Practices like meditation, prayer, visualization, journaling, or sacred writing are great tools for embracing change and transformation. Working with a success coach, therapist, hypnotherapist, NLP practitioner, or EFT coach (tapping) can also be valuable on a healing journey. These methods focus on taking responsibility for our healing and being proactive in our transformation.

The Continuous Journey of Transformation

In conclusion, the journey of transformation is deeply personal and unique to each individual. Whether prompted by loss, a conscious decision, or an unexpected life event, the process of inner revolution requires courage, resilience, and a willingness to embrace change. As we navigate through grief and the challenges that arise, it is essential to honor our emotions and allow ourselves to fully heal.

By doing so, we create space for growth, discovering new strengths and insights that can guide us towards achieving our own definition of greatness. By fostering an attitude of positivity and expectancy, we can step into our greatness and live a life filled with purpose, joy, and wholeness.

Transformation is not a destination but a continuous journey, shaped by our experiences and choices. As we move forward, let us trust in our ability to navigate change, embrace our emotions, and uncover the hidden opportunities within our challenges. This opens us to the possibility of a richer, more fulfilling life, grounded in our true selves and aligned with our deepest values and aspirations.

The journey of transformation, particularly through the lens of loss and grief, is deeply personal and varied. As explored in this chapter, the essence of genuine change lies within us—an "inside job" that calls for courage and introspection. We must define our own greatness and pursue it with a sense of inner strength, acknowledging that life's inevitable disruptions can serve as powerful catalysts for growth.

By facing our emotions head-on and allowing ourselves to grieve fully, we create the space necessary for healing and resilience to emerge. Whether through spiritual practices, therapeutic or holistic modalities, or simply the willingness to explore alternative paths, the tools for achieving greatness are within our reach.

About Donna Baranyay

Donna Baranyay is a seasoned Grief and Spirituality Coach, bringing over 15 years of experience in supporting individuals through the challenges of loss, change, and spiritual growth. As the founder of Our Sacred Journeys, she is committed to providing compassionate guidance to those navigating grief, embracing change, and seeking spiritual transformation.

With a diverse educational background that includes Transform Destiny, Emerson Theological Institute, and the University of Metaphysics, Donna holds certifications in Hypnotherapy and Coaching. She also earned her Certificate in Thanatology from the Association of Death Education and Counseling, allowing her to offer tailored insights and strategies for each individual's journey from healing to thriving.

Passionate about helping others through their unique paths, Donna encourages clients to rediscover their inherent gifts. Through her compassionate guidance, she inspires them to face life with resilience and grace while finding renewed meaning and purpose.

To get Donna's gift, visit:

www.InnerRevolutionBook.com/gift/Donna

Transformation is not a destination but a continuous journey, shaped by our experiences and choices.

Inner Revolution: Embracing Change to Achieve Greatness

Achieving Greatness within Your Relationships

Nadirah & Troy Lugg, Transformation Experts

Troy's Perspective

Anticipation: The "Honey, I Got This" Moment

It was one of those calm Sunday mornings in Chicago. The smell of coffee filled the kitchen and there was this precious silence. The kind that only happens before Nadirah wakes up. But today, I anticipated Nadirah's next move. I knew that as soon as she got out of bed, she'd head to the bathroom and beeline to the closet to find something "appropriate" for their Sunday Brunch with family. The problem? I had forgotten to pick up the dry cleaning.

But this wasn't my first rodeo. I learned that a good husband anticipates problems before they become disasters. Grabbing my keys, I sped to the dry cleaners, praying they were open.

Twenty minutes later, with a bag of freshly pressed clothes, I entered the house just in time for Nadirah to emerge from the bedroom. I stood there holding her favorite outfit.

"Good morning, babe," I said, acting cool.

Nadirah looked at me with that knowing smile. "Nice save."

Lesson Learned: Anticipation in marriage is about staying ahead of the game and knowing what the other person needs, even before they do.

Navigation: The Road Trip of Marriage

Every married couple knows that a road trip will test your love in creative ways. Nadirah and I were no exception. On the way to a getaway, we found ourselves in the dreaded situation: lost, hungry, and tired.

I swore I knew a "shortcut." Spoiler alert: I didn't, but I thought I did.

"I'm telling you, Nadirah, just trust me. This is going to cut at least 30 minutes off the drive," I said with my eyes glued to the GPS, which was conveniently offline.

But after an hour of winding roads, Nadirah's eyebrows had ascended to record-breaking heights. "Troy, this looks like the set of a horror movie."

Of course, we ended up at a dead-end, but it was a turning point for me in more ways than one. I pulled over, took a deep breath, and finally said, "Alright, babe. You lead."

That's when I realized marriage is a journey, and sometimes it's better to trust your partner's navigation skills. After all, Nadirah always had the uncanny ability to find the right path (both literally and figuratively).

Lesson Learned: Sometimes, to navigate life successfully, let someone else take the wheel.

Communication: The "You Said What?" Dance

I believed I was a fantastic communicator... until Nadirah proved otherwise.

One evening, we were hosting friends, and I confidently told everyone, "Nadirah loves my cooking. She told me last week she could eat my salmon every day."

Cue Nadirah's laugh. "Um... what I actually said was, 'I could not eat your salmon every day. I need variety.'"

The room and my face went silent.

Communication, I learned that day, was about listening to what was said, repeating back to make sure everything was correctly understood, and clarifying when things got lost in translation.

Before assuming anything, I learned to ask, "Is that what you meant?" It saved me from many future "salmon situations."

Lesson Learned: Clear, two-way communication is key in marriage.

Listen & Learn: The Double-L Challenge

Listening wasn't my strong suit when I first got married. I was a "fixer." Every time Nadirah talked about her day, I was ready with solutions.

One day, Nadirah came home from work frustrated about a meeting. I jumped in with, "You should just tell them to…"

"Hold on," Nadirah interrupted. "I don't need a solution, Troy. I just need you to listen."

It was a wake-up call. I realized Nadirah wanted a partner who would be present to truly hear her out. Listening wasn't just about hearing and waiting for your turn to speak; it was about showing you care enough to understand.

Lesson Learned: Listening and learning go hand in hand, and often, your partner is just asking for your ear.

Lead: The Quiet Power of Stepping Up

In our marriage, I prided myself on being a leader. But as the years passed, I realized leading was about stepping up when needed and letting Nadirah shine when it was her turn.

One memorable day, we had a big decision to make about moving to California for Nadirah's career. I was nervous, unsure about leaving behind everything familiar. But Nadirah was excited and ready to leap.

I thought long and hard before saying, "Let's do it. I'll support you 100%."

At that moment, I realized leadership was about showing my greatness by supporting my partner's greatness. It was about leading with love versus ego. That's when I knew that our marriage was strong, because of what we've accomplished together.

<u>Lesson Learned</u>: True leadership in marriage is stepping up when necessary and stepping back to let your partner shine when it's their time.

By using anticipation, navigation, communication, listening, learning, and leading, I learned to show my greatness not only to myself but to others through my marriage. And Nadirah? Well, she always knew that next to every great man is a woman who's got the map, the directions, and occasionally the dry-cleaning ticket.

Nadirah's Perspective

Anticipation: The Power of Expecting the Unexpected

I always prided myself on being able to anticipate things. I predicted that our key to success was rooted in a move from Chicago to California or when Troy would discover my hidden stash of snacks. But anticipating marriage life was another story.

One evening, Troy came home to find me sitting on the couch with a particular look in my eyes—the kind that said, "We need to talk." I could tell by his expression that Troy's mind was racing, wondering if he'd forgotten an anniversary, or left his socks in the wrong place. But I remembered this first life lesson: anticipation.

He didn't rush in with assumptions or excuses. Instead, he calmly sat down next to me, prepared for whatever was coming his way.

"Troy, I want to go back to school and get my master's degree."

A smile crept across Troy's face. Both Troy and I learned it wasn't just about bracing for big moments, it was about anticipating the little things, the everyday surprises that come along with sharing your life with someone else. Anticipation isn't about control, it's about readiness.

<u>Embracing change</u> *with the readiness to adapt, to flow freely like water, and to show greatness by rolling with the unexpected, understanding that it will lead to something greater.*

Navigation: The Art of Steering the Ship

Raised in a single-parent household during my early childhood, I quickly learned the importance of doing things right and becoming self-reliant. So initially, I thought marriage was like driving a car. Keep your eyes on the road, steer the wheel, check in with your copilot, and you'll be fine, right? Wrong. Marriage, I quickly learned, was more like navigating a ship through a stormy sea. There were days of smooth sailing, but every so often, a wave would come out of nowhere and shake the boat. That's where Troy came in.

Troy had this incredible knack for seeing things I didn't see, as he's a big-picture thinker. While I'm more into the details of any situation or solution. That happens a lot in relationships. One person may have a gift for an area of life, while your partner has a special gift in another area.

The blessing is that you figure out whose natural gift will best serve the particular situation. When we hit rough waters, Troy would calmly adjust the sails, helping us navigate through whatever storm was brewing; be it finances, family, or the most dangerous of all: assembling IKEA furniture together.

I realized that leadership in marriage was about knowing when to let your partner take the helm of the ship. And sometimes, it was about checking in to make sure we were both looking at the same map.

<u>Embracing change</u> by believing that navigation is about charting a course together.

Communication: The Unseen Superpower

It was a Saturday morning when Troy surprised me with breakfast. He carefully prepared a seafood omelet, French toast, and poured my favorite juice. But when I walked into the kitchen, sat at the table, and grabbed my fork and knife, I stared at the table, then at Troy.

"Umm... did you forget the syrup?"

Troy stared back, his mind suddenly blank. How could he have missed the syrup? It was the finishing touch!

That's when I said, with a grin, "I love you for the effort made."

And just like that, Troy and I both learned that communication in marriage was about the messages you send saying nothing at all. It was the way I smiled at his effort, and that it was about the fact that he put forth a compassionate gesture. Over breakfast, communication was more than just talking. It was understanding each other's love language and knowing when a simple "I love you" could smooth over any forgotten condiment.

<u>Embracing change</u> by me feeling the sweetness of his heart and by him seeing the joy expressed by my heart that made that breakfast even more delicious without the syrup.

Listening: The Secret Ingredient

One evening, as we sat on our patio together, I began telling Troy about my exhausting and frustrating day. Troy listened for about five minutes before jumping in with solutions.

"You should've just told them no. And maybe if you rearrange your schedule..."

But I stopped him with a knowing look. "Troy, I already have a solution. I just needed you to listen to me."

That hit Troy like a ton of bricks, but he understood the assignment, as we both have been guilty of the savior complex to help others, even when no one asked for help. I was taking a moment to share my experience and feelings with someone who would listen with a nonjudgmental ear.

We've learned throughout our marriage that listening is about being present versus just about hearing words.

Embracing change, realizing that sometimes greatness, in any relationship, is as simple as closing your mouth and opening your heart. And maybe, after the venting session, ask if the other person is looking for a solution.

Learning: The Journey Never Ends

With a background in teaching, I have always considered myself a lifelong learner, and marriage has been the most educational experience of them all. Every day I spend with my husband, I'm learning a new lesson, and Troy has been the best teacher and student I've ever had.

Throughout time, I've learned that it's not enough to just know things. You also have to apply the wisdom. It's about being better versus being right. I've learned from triumphs and challenges, the laughter, and the tears, that marriage isn't a destination but a continuous journey of growth. I am not the same person Troy met 35 years ago in elementary school and vice versa. We learn, evolve, elevate, and share our wisdom with others along the way.

Embracing change requires acceptance that greatness is gained by learning from your mistakes, recognizing the signs of a similar future situation, applying what you've learned, and doing better the next time around.

Leading: A Partnership in Progress

If there was one thing I've learned about leadership, it was this: true leadership in marriage is about serving, about lifting each other versus being the boss or tearing each other down for rank or status. I knew I had strengths, but so did Troy. And together, we had to love, heal, repair, and rebuild. We embraced change in where we lived, family dynamics, communication, and love language, in order to lead by example. Not just for each other, but for everyone around us.

People often ask, "What's your secret?" And Troy and I often smile and say, "We've learned to clearly communicate and lead each other."

Troy and I didn't have all the answers, but together, we've created a partnership built on mutual respect, love, trust, and communication. We've purposefully shared with the world that marriage is about walking side by side, lifting each other when one stumbled, and celebrating together when we've reached new heights.

Overall, that was the greatness Troy, and I had discovered. Not in being perfect, but in perfectly *embracing change* to flow and learn the previously mentioned lessons. A greatness that has made our love not just something to cherish, but something worth respecting and honoring for a lifetime.

About Nadirah & Troy Lugg

Nadirah Lugg (Your Clarity Queen) earned a B.A. in Speech Communication from the University of Illinois and an M.A. in Liberal Arts from the University of Chicago. She is also a certified Clarity Coach, Yoga Instructor, Clinical Hypnotherapist, Reiki Master, published author, trained astrologer, intuitive Tarot card reader, inspirational medium speaker, singer/songwriter, and actress. Nadirah loves empowering women who are navigating grief and coaches innovative ways to communicate with their transitioned loved ones through an engaging and holistic approach.

Troy Lugg is a renowned motivational speaker and elite safety professional, making a significant impact on the American workforce and family. His unique approach and passion for helping others empower thousands to realize their potential. Holding both a Bachelor's and Master's degree in Industrial Management, with an emphasis on Safety, Troy is dedicated to his craft. As he continues his journey to become the world's #1 motivational speaker, he looks forward to sharing his inspiring story and insights with audiences everywhere.

Get a free gift from Nadirah and Troy by visiting:

www.InnerRevolutionBook.com/gift/Nadirah-Troy

Inner Revolution: Embracing Change to Achieve Greatness

Transforming Pain into Purpose
Michael Roth, C. Ad, SRC

If you're reading this, odds are you've suffered the torturing pain of trauma. Maybe you still are, maybe you even coach others through it. I'm Michael Roth and I've been a Neuro-Linguistic Programming (NLP) Master Practitioner and Trainer for over 40 years. What impresses me repeatedly about NLP is how reprogramming negative thought patterns releases the energy of trauma that has been stored in the body.

NLP techniques help reset the nervous system, allowing the body to release stored pain and promoting healing from within. As my practice grew, I observed that a common side effect of trauma is a diminished sense of self-worth. To address this, I incorporated lessons on confidence, authoritative communication, and leadership into my coaching. I found that trauma survivors often possess a unique understanding of spiritual truth, which not only helps them achieve a new level of strength but also inspires and heals those around them.

A Two-Step Approach to Trauma

This has become my unique two-step approach to trauma: first, reset the nervous system and free the person from trauma's crippling grip; then second, fill the space that trauma occupied with confidence, speaking truth, and leadership skills. I realize that trauma survivors are the actual teachers and leaders our planet so desperately needs and that now is the time to show up.

So that we're on the same page, let me share some definitions with you. Trauma is talked about more and more often, especially since 2020, but let's get clear on what trauma is actually referring to.

Trauma is a deeply distressing experience that overwhelms an individual's ability to cope. It affects not only the mind but also the body, creating a long-lasting impact on mental, emotional, and physical health. Trauma can arise from various sources, including emotional, physical, sexual, or psychological abuse; neglect; accidents; or unexpected losses. It may result from a singular event or prolonged exposure to distress, such as childhood abuse or chronic illness. Trauma is a deeply personal experience; what feels traumatic for one person may not be the same for another.

While the brain and body are naturally equipped to handle stress, trauma overwhelms the nervous system, sometimes trapping individuals in a "survival mode" state. Even when the external threat has passed, the mind and body may continue to react as if the danger is still present, resulting in chronic stress, anxiety, or dissociation.

Types of Traumas:

- Acute Trauma: Trauma stemming from a single, overwhelming event, such as an accident or natural disaster.

- Chronic Trauma: Prolonged exposure to high-stress situations, such as ongoing abuse or long-term neglect.
- Complex Trauma: Multiple, varied traumatic events over time, often involving betrayal or a violation of trust in personal relationships, such as in cases of childhood abuse.

Trauma and Process Addictions

A key focus of my work has been addressing unresolved trauma to release process addictions—non-substance addictions such as gambling, sex, love addiction, and intimacy anorexia—where one actively withholds emotional, spiritual, and sexual intimacy from their partner. People often rely on addictive behaviors to manage intense emotions or to numb the pain that trauma can cause.

Rather than being the primary issue, addiction serves as a coping mechanism, a symptom of deeper emotional wounds. For many, addiction is an attempt to self-medicate in response to the lasting impact of trauma, creating cycles of avoidance and self-destructive behavior. Addressing the root trauma can pave the way to lasting recovery and healing.

The traditional approach to trauma treatment often focuses on talk therapy and medication, which address the mind. However, trauma also penetrates the body, which is why incorporating mind-body techniques is essential.

I've had the privilege of learning from masters of mind-body healing and have witnessed firsthand how powerful the mind-body connection can be in addressing trauma. I've created a unique blend of processes that are very effective in helping individuals release their significant emotional events, allowing them to live life with freedom, peace of mind, and purpose.

These Processes Include:

1. **Neuro-Linguistic Programming (NLP):** NLP works by helping individuals reframe and reprogram negative thought patterns that result from traumatic experiences. NLP emphasizes the connection between how we think, the language we use, and how we behave. For individuals struggling with addiction or trauma, NLP can help shift the meaning they've attached to their traumatic experiences and alter their emotional and behavioral responses.

By using NLP techniques like reframing and anchoring, I help individuals break free from self-limiting beliefs and responses that were formed by trauma. This approach effectively helps individuals reshape their relationship with traumatic memories, ultimately building emotional resilience.

2. **Emotional Freedom Techniques (EFT):** EFT, also known as tapping, combines elements of acupressure and cognitive-behavioral therapy. Tapping on specific meridian points while focusing on the trauma helps release the emotional energy stored in the body. EFT is a practical tool for reducing anxiety, stress, and emotional overwhelm.

By coaching individuals to tap on acupressure points while recalling distressing memories, they can release blocked energy in the body, which reduces the emotional intensity of the trauma. EFT has been shown to lower cortisol levels, calm the nervous system, and help manage stress responses more effectively.

3. **Havening Techniques:** Havening is a psychosensory technique that uses touch to reset the brain's response to traumatic memories. Guiding an individual through gentle touches to the face, arms, or hands during recall of a traumatic event causes changes in the brain's pathways, leading to the desensitization of the emotional response associated with the memory.

Havening promotes the release of serotonin and other neurotransmitters that play a key role in calming the brain and reducing the intensity of trauma. Over time, havening can help the nervous system shift from a state of heightened alert to one of relaxation and balance.

4. **Eye Movement Integration (EMI):** EMI is a trauma treatment technique I use that helps integrate fragmented memories by using specific eye movement patterns. EMI encourages the brain to reprocess traumatic memories in a way that reduces their emotional charge. Guiding the eyes through specific movements helps the brain more effectively integrate and process traumatic experiences.

This integration helps individuals become less emotionally reactive to the trauma, allowing them to recall painful memories without being overwhelmed by distressing feelings.

5. **Somatic Experiencing (SE):** SE directly engages the body to help release stored trauma. Through this technique, I guide individuals to focus on their bodily sensations rather than relying only on talking through traumatic events. Trauma often causes individuals to disconnect from their bodies, and SE gently guides them back to an awareness of physical sensations, enabling the nervous system to discharge stored tension.

Being led to give attention to these sensations in a safe and supported environment, allows one to release them, and the nervous system can regain its natural rhythm. SE is effective in healing trauma-related symptoms such as chronic pain, tension, and physical dissociation.

6. **Polyvagal Theory and Vagal Nerve Stimulation:** The Polyvagal Theory highlights the role of the vagus nerve, the main nerve of the parasympathetic nervous system, in regulating our physiological responses to trauma. Trauma can disrupt vagal tone, leading to an overactive sympathetic nervous system and the fight-or-flight response. Polyvagal-informed practices, such as deep breathing, chanting, and humming, can stimulate the vagus nerve and activate the parasympathetic nervous system, promoting calm and recovery.

The nervous system plays a pivotal role in how we experience and recover from trauma. When trauma occurs, the body's natural stress-response system is often overwhelmed, causing individuals to remain stuck in a state of hyperarousal. I've found restoring vagal tone is critical for individuals with trauma, as it allows the body to return to a state of safety and calm, ultimately enabling the healing process.

A Comprehensive Approach to Healing

The combination of techniques I use discussed above—NLP, EFT, Havening, EMI, Somatic Experiencing, and Polyvagal Theory—reset the nervous system by helping it shift from a state of hyperarousal and fight-or-flight to one of calm and recovery, or rest and digest.

I specifically focus on these approaches because they facilitate healing by addressing both the mental and physical components of trauma. Many trauma survivors carry emotional pain in their bodies, which manifests as tension, chronic pain, or digestive issues. By working with the body and mind together, I help my clients achieve a more complete recovery and the ability to move into an expanded way of living.

I came to realize that after my clients survived the mental, physical, and emotional pain of their trauma, they still had residual shame, guilt, and other forms of self-judgment. As we explored this, I discovered many had incurred profound insights, beliefs, and practices they'd used to help them remain whole enough to seek coaching and recover from their traumatic experience. But because of the impact of their trauma, they'd felt afraid to express their unique voice.

By encouraging individuals to harness the courage they developed while navigating their trauma and to honor their true selves, I help them discover what truly matters to them and why. They then create talks, classes, and workshops to share these insights. As a result, these individuals emerge as the teachers, ministers, healers, counselors, and voices that our world needs. They inspire others who are struggling with personal trauma and the weight of current events to seek coaching, embrace recovery, and become unique voices of healing.

Transforming Pain into Purpose

What keeps me excited and dedicated after 40 years of supporting individuals in their recovery from trauma is that healing trauma is a multi-layered process, requiring a comprehensive approach addressing both the mind and body. While traditional therapies are important, incorporating mind-body techniques like NLP, EFT, Havening, EMI, Somatic Experiencing, and Polyvagal stimulation ensures that trauma survivors experience deep, lasting healing. And providing individuals with self-honor, confidence, speaking, and leadership skills helps them move beyond surviving to inspiring and healing others.

Through the combination of processes I employ, individuals can release their emotional pain, reset their nervous systems, and rediscover the ability to live a life of peace, freedom, and purpose. Addressing trauma holistically allows individuals not only to survive but to thrive. Providing ways for them to express all they've learned from their trauma allows them to stand solid as who and what they are, and then to inspire others. The road to recovery may be challenging, but with the right tools and guidance, it is entirely possible to break free from the grip of trauma and live a life of courage and purpose.

If this chapter resonated with you and you're interested in exploring a path forward together, reach out at HolisticTraumaTransformation@gmail.com. Mention this chapter, and we'll arrange a complimentary 15-minute conversation to discuss what our work together could be like. I look forward to connecting with you and supporting your journey.

About Michael Roth

Michael Roth, C. Ad, SRC, is a Holistic Addiction and Wellness Specialist, Life Coach, author, and speaker with over 40 years of experience. He is dedicated to helping individuals break free from trauma and addictions, particularly sex, love, and gambling addictions.

Through a holistic approach emphasizing the mind-body connection, Michael works with clients globally via confidential online methods, offering a pathway to hope, healing, and lasting transformation.

His passion for this work stems from his own personal journey. Growing up in a family shrouded in secrecy, he faced addiction firsthand, experiencing shame, guilt, and the consequences of his choices. Now, he channels that empathy and understanding into his practice.

While Michael holds numerous certifications, including Addictionologist (C. Ad) and Sexual Addiction Recovery Coach (SRC), his focus remains on helping clients find hope and healing. His innovative, research-backed methods empower individuals to reclaim their lives and overcome addiction.

Get Michael's gift here:

www.InnerRevolutionBook.com/gift/Michael

Addressing trauma holistically allows individuals not only to survive but to thrive.

Inner Revolution: Embracing Change to Achieve Greatness

Embracing Change to Achieve Greatness

Carolyn Cahn, RN, MHA, CCHt

We absorb what we hear, both the good and the bad. And whether true or not, if you hear something enough times, you start to believe it.

Research increasingly shows that children exposed to adverse childhood experiences often face challenges in adulthood. These experiences, including physical or emotional abuse, sexual abuse, or witnessing violence at home or in their community, can leave lasting effects. However, the way these hard events impact each child can differ significantly.

One way that a child is affected by what happens to them, or around them, is to internalize what they hear, see, and feel. Feeling poorly about oneself is fairly common, and internalizing the negative emotions can result. A child will believe the negatives and will incorporate these planted ideas, hence creating negative self-talk.

Negative self-talk is when you think or say bad things about yourself, like "I'm not good enough" or "I always mess up." It's like having a very mean voice inside your head that makes you feel sad or discouraged.

My story is proof of how others can mess with your head and create a person with negative thoughts. It also proves that you can redefine yourself and become the person you want to be.

From an early age, the message was clear: I was not enough. Not smart enough, not religious enough, not thin enough, not rich enough. Dumb. Lazy. These labels followed me everywhere, both at school and at home, echoing through my thoughts and shaping how I saw myself.

My parents met and married in New York City. After having two children and living in a one-room apartment, my dad bought a neighborhood delicatessen. My mother, never expecting to work seven days a week, was not happy with her lot in life.

To ensure a better education, I was enrolled in a parochial school thanks to scholarships. For eight years, I was in the smaller of the three classes, known lovingly as the "dumb class." We were the students who were deemed not smart enough for either the average or the accelerated classes. I would come home to hear my mother call me dumb, lazy, and fat.

My grades reflected a school system that treated all children the same, despite learning challenges. I was frustrated and bored at school. Then I entered a public high school where I continued to struggle through four years of poor grades.

I did not know how to study, and I never learned how to memorize information. Despite this, I was extremely motivated to go to college for two powerful reasons. First was that every single friend went to college after high school. My second reason was that I did not want to wind up like my parents, who worked so hard for so little. I believed college was my only option after high school, even though my parents couldn't afford to pay for it.

Nursing sounded like a good choice to me because after two years of college, I could support myself. Living in New York City with its great transportation system made it possible to work in an office and take night classes at a community college. I got a nursing degree from a community college and started working to support my educational goals. I got a bachelor's degree in nursing and a Master of Health Service Administration.

In my early 40s my best friend, another survivor of the elementary school's "dumb class," called me to explain that she figured out what was wrong with us; we both had ADHD. She had done research and put the pieces together. I then went to a psychiatrist to verify this diagnosis. Now I have an explanation for all the challenges I had in school.

The educational system in many areas of the country, and the world, is not adept at identifying mental and physical challenges. Even when a diagnosis is made, many schools lack the funding to provide the necessary resources for every student.

Another challenge is that parents often refuse to acknowledge or accept that their child has a problem. This can cause adverse childhood experiences, adding to the existing challenges.

I have learned the value of having a clear goal and surrounding yourself with the right people to help you achieve those goals. For me, doing things in bite-sized pieces was my way of succeeding in school. I never took over nine college credits at one time to ensure that I was not overloaded mentally and started with a two-year community college, ensured that I would have a way to support myself.

Setting clear achievable goals allows you to have a higher chance of success. And once you succeed in something you have never done before, the emotional success and reinforcement in your brain fuels self-confidence. When you feel good about one thing, you can apply success to other areas of life. And the more success you have, the easier positive self-talk becomes.

College may not be for you, but regardless of what you did in your life, success in any area will boost your self-confidence. Build on that success and continue to work on positive self-talk to move you forward in your life.

Nursing requires that we take continuing education courses. There was a flier on the bulletin board at work announcing a three-day seminar on hypnosis for nursing credits. That is how I came to be in the classroom of Dr. A.M. Krassner, creator of the Krasner Method of hypnotherapy. His work introduced me to the power of the subconscious mind and how direct suggestions could create positive change. It was through this association that I was introduced to Tad James and neurolinguistics. Years later, I got my Neuro-Linguistic Practitioner Certification (NLP) and other certifications.

Through this work, I came to understand how persistent your brain's inner chatter can alter who you are. You can become a successful person in an area you never dreamed possible, or you can self-destruct and face negative patterns that prevent your living your best life. If you say things enough times, your brain will incorporate this, and that is who or what you will become.

Growing up, I had unconsciously made the choice to accept the negativity of others, and I repeated those negative messages through my inner monologue or self-talk. I knew that to change my life trajectory, I had to shift my thinking into positive thoughts, statements, and actions.

The first step to shifting away from negative self-talk is to recognize it when it happens. As an example, imagine that you are driving on a freeway and miss the turnoff, and you think or say, "I'm so stupid" or "What an idiot." As soon as a negative thought comes into your mind, stop. Change it to a positive statement that you can believe in, like "I need to pay more attention when I'm driving" or "Oops, what is the next exit that I can take?"

Consider the situation of missing an important appointment. Instead of dwelling on negative thoughts, you can reframe your mindset with positive statements, such as, "How can I prevent this from happening again?" or "I should call them right away to explain."

It is common for people to reflect on something that didn't go as planned, and the negative, destructive self-talk begins. As you catch yourself starting on this self-defeating talk, stop. Change it to something positive like, "People always make mistakes, so how can I fix this?" You can also say, "I made a mistake, but let me call someone who can help me fix this."

Once you figured out how to fix the error, you can reinforce the positive. The next time you make a mistake, pause, and remind yourself that you're human. Embrace the challenge, and approach fixing it with excitement as a fun opportunity for growth.

Journaling is a great way to reflect on your negative self-talk. Think about negative thoughts you had that day and then write at least one positive response for each one in the journal. Writing in a journal has so many benefits, but you should handwrite with a pen or pencil, and not a computer or cell phone. When you write, it is more deliberate and requires more concentration. In addition, writing involves the use of fine motor skills that activate various parts of your brain.

Another effective strategy is to ask friends and family to point out when you make a negative statement. When they bring it to your attention, thank them and immediately make a positive statement to replace it. As an example, while you are driving with a friend, you drive through a red light without stopping. Instead of using creative negative statements, you can say, "Thankfully, there was no other car." Or "I'd better pay more attention to my driving," or even "Thankfully, there were no police around."

Having clear goals can also help with changing self-talk to more positive thinking. The more you accomplish, the more reinforcement that you can do what you set out to do.

You can do little things to help others, like "pay-it-forward." Paying the toll for the person behind you can be fun! I remember being in a 99 Cent store looking for something. A woman who was still wearing her work name tag started talking to me. Based upon her statements, she was counting her pennies. I walked away, pulled out a twenty-dollar bill and walked back to the woman, saying that she could now buy those items she wanted. The smile on her face lit my heart.

Later, I found myself filled with uplifting thoughts and positive self-talk. I rarely share when I do things like this because I don't do it for myself. The positive feedback I get from the action alone helps me feel amazing, and it doesn't have to involve money. Try it one day when you are not feeling great and see how turning your attention outside of yourself can lift your energy.

Have you ever faced the challenge of trying something new? Instead of allowing yourself to doubt your abilities, you can boost your confidence by saying things like, "I have done things like this before," or "I am up for this challenge!" Every time you succeed in a new venture, your self-confidence increases. This is true regardless of whether you learn to drive a stick shift, sky dive out of a plane or run a marathon. Challenging yourself and succeeding creates significant positive energy and makes thinking about yourself in a more positive way easier.

Remember that you may not always be in control or have control in a situation. When I worked for the government, there were so many rules and regulations and I would get very frustrated, especially when I failed to accomplish what I wanted to do. Once I had a clear plan, I learned to present it to my boss and ask, "Is this something I can do?" If given a green light, I would push forward with positive energy and a clear goal. If, however, I was told that this plan could not be implemented, I would look to see if there was another way to achieve the desired outcome. Sometimes, we can't do exactly what we want, so understanding what is realistically possible can help you avoid certain or likely failure.

I achieved success because I surrounded myself with positive people. By realizing who you are, where you are, and acknowledging your strengths and weaknesses, you will allow yourself to move forward in life. By telling yourself that things are possible and creating a clear path forward, you can achieve amazing things, even if there are roadblocks along the way.

Remember that change happens with inner work, clarity, persistence, and consistency. Learning to care for yourself, and even love yourself, takes time and patience. Practice this until positive self-talk becomes a habit.

Also, be sure to set both short-term and long-term goals. This allows you to measure your success and provides you with additional opportunities for positive self-talk. It is important to review your goals frequently so that you move forward in the direction you choose. It's like your car's GPS; if you don't set it with a specific address, you might turn off on the wrong street and wind up far from your original destination.

Embracing the ability to change your self-talk will redefine your life. Instead of letting negative and destructive thoughts dictate your actions and self-worth, you can build a foundation of positive affirmations and hopeful perspectives that empower you to achieve your goals. Whether it is navigating a challenging career, overcoming personal obstacles, or simply striving to be a better person each day, it begins with what you say to yourself.

The journey to transformation is within your grasp, one positive thought at a time.

About Carolyn Cahn

Carolyn Cahn is a seasoned Success Coach and Registered Nurse with over 25 years of experience in empowering adults to transform their lives. With degrees from George Washington University and Alfred University, along with certifications in NLP, Coaching, Hypnosis, Medical Hypnosis and Stage Hypnosis from Dr. A.M. Krasner, The Tad James Company, American Institute of Hypnotherapy and others, Carolyn combines a wealth of knowledge with practical expertise.

Specializing in guiding individuals who are burned out or seeking change, she helps clients release negative experiences and achieve their personal and professional goals. By utilizing Integral Eye Movement Therapy (IEMT), Carolyn effectively assists clients in overcoming emotional hurdles linked to challenging memories.

In her impressive career, Carolyn has managed 18 clinics and collaborated with various companies to foster healthier workplaces. She is dedicated to helping individuals harness their strengths to tackle challenges such as low self-esteem, ADHD, and burnout, leading them to a more fulfilling life.

To get Carolyn's gift, visit:

www.InnerRevolutionBook.com/gift/Carolyn

Embracing the ability to change your self-talk will redefine your life.

Inner Revolution: Embracing Change to Achieve Greatness

It's Your Choice

Brandy Lovingier, NLPP, PTT, CCHt, CSC, Reiki Master Trainer

Sometimes, the negative things you say to yourself did not start with you. These thoughts may come from the situations you were born into, starting in childhood, shaped by the troubles, judgments, and decisions placed on you by others.

Maybe you also heard phrases like, "You'll never amount to anything," "You're a mistake," or "You're a problem." These weren't your thoughts, but believing them may have made your life harder than it needed to be.

Letting other people's problems infect your mind can be damaging. Maybe you're in a place where you talk negatively to yourself. What truly matters isn't who said these things, what they said, or why they said them. What matters is your choice to carry, believe, and hold on to hurtful words that serve no purpose.

No matter when your negative self-talk started—whether in childhood, school, marriage or at work—knowing that you have control over what you believe is key to breaking free. Remember, no one can break you without your permission. It's your choice.

Be Your Own Hero

I'm a very caring person, and I'm also honest and direct. No one is coming to save you, and relying on others for your happiness won't bring you the joy or fulfillment that you seek. Challenges and tough times are a part of life and can help you grow if you face them head-on. These experiences also make you more compassionate, which is something our world really needs.

If you change your perspective to see things as happening for you, instead of to you, you can truly improve yourself. Thinking in a victim sense, with thoughts like "This happened to me, so..." will only cause more problems and hardships. I know bad things happen, and I feel for you because I understand how stressful and painful they can be. But staying in that victim-effect mindset or state won't help you.

Genuine change takes work. It involves thinking, taking responsibility, planning, and then acting. Tell yourself, "This event happened. How did I play a part in it? What can I learn from it? Yes, it was hard and awful! Now, what can I do to move forward for my own good?" Be your own hero and stand up for yourself.

Mindset and The Empty Pavement

Your mindset affects EVERYTHING. Are you looking for solutions, or are you fighting to stay stuck in your problems? If you're finding yourself stuck, remember you can only get over things by facing them head-on. It's important to understand your feelings and let them out instead of hiding them. You have to deal with your problems to move on and let them go. What you focus on in life will grow, whether it's good or bad.

I remember when I was in my early 20s, my car got stolen in St. Louis. My boyfriend at the time was shocked and asked, "What are you going to do?" I said, "Well, staring at the empty pavement won't get me anywhere, will it?" Then I started looking for a new car. Whatever is happening in your life, are you just staring at the empty pavement?

Change your focus and think differently. Think about the saying, "If I knew then what I know now." So, imagine yourself at 99 years old, looking back on your life now. What advice would you give yourself? For me, it would be, "Stop wasting time and get on with your life!"

The good news is, you don't have to look back with regret. You can make changes now! Forgive yourself for the past, because it's never too late to begin again. Listen to your future, older, wiser self. Close your eyes and really listen. Then promise to live your life to the fullest for yourself.

Power Placement

Who or what you give your power to is important. Setting boundaries and confidently saying no is essential. The standards you set for yourself and others shape your personal space. Be aware of your surroundings and be ready to change your environment or the people you spend time with if needed. It's perfectly okay to distance yourself from bad influences and situations, even if they are friends or family.

When I married my husband, I thought gaining a new family would be wonderful! I imagined having a mom, dad, and siblings who loved me. Since I lost my core family earlier than most, I was truly looking forward to this. But it didn't turn out that way, and that's ok. Even as an adult, you can still hear, "You don't belong." Be thankful you don't.

I was giving too much power to something that didn't help me but hurt me. Should I give my power away, staying sad and angry? Or should I keep my power and be thankful that I don't belong to that way of thinking? I'll keep my power and choose to be thankful.

It's important to know the difference between running away from something and moving towards a safer, healthier space for yourself. Being conflict-avoidant, staying silent, and doing nothing will not change or improve your situation. Reflect and confront the areas of your life that aren't healthy for you and take action.

If there is no positive change, it's time to remove those toxic influences from your life. This is about knowing your worth and keeping your power. This could be exactly what you need to start positive change and momentum for yourself.

Hate vs. Compassion

Trust me, it's really hard when you feel you've had enough. You run out of patience and feel you need to let out all your anger. "RELEASE THE KRAKEN!" That's what it feels like for me, anyway. The she-beast from the deep is coming to the surface. Look out!

It's okay to realize that someone might not be right for you or that you just don't click with them. I teach this very thing to my daughter, who is being treated poorly by a girl in her class. You don't have to be friends with or like everyone. That's ok, and it's not reality, anyway. But you don't have to be mean either or hate people. Holding onto hate will only hurt you in the end.

I'm not just someone who talks about ways to improve life and guides others through the process; I've applied these steps on my journey. Letting go of hate and anger was possible for me by embracing compassion and sympathy.

How? When someone treats you poorly, view them as sad, lost and still trying to find their way. Stay away, keeping your distance from them, but still care about them and wish them well. Feel sorry for them and be grateful for what you have and who you are, instead of hating them. Wish them well on their journey in life because they still have a lot to learn.

You are at your own unique point in personal growth, just like everyone else is at theirs. You can't expect others to be where you are, and they can't expect you to be where they are. Focus on your journey, your growth, the life you want to live, and the person you want to become. Some people may try to bring you down, but keep your distance, wish them well, and approach the situation with compassion.

Connect To Yourself

Now is the moment to truly recognize and accept who you are. There is only one magnificent, wonderful you. You are unique, and how you value, respect, and see yourself will affect... well, everything.

Maybe it's time to reconnect with yourself? What does that look like? Seek the good and find all those things to be thankful for. I usually list three at the end of my daily meditation. There is always something to be profoundly grateful for. Discover it.

Ground yourself by spending time outdoors, taking a walk in nature, or indulging in deep breaths during a warm bubble bath. Spend time with animals. Nourish your soul. Engage in activities you love weekly, whether it's roller skating, hiking, creating art, or any craft that speaks to you. Fit it into your schedule and revitalize yourself. This is of utmost importance.

Start small by listing the things you'd like to change in your life and the things you desire for yourself. Review your current schedule and adjust it to make room for these positive new habits or activities you promise to yourself. Do you break promises to others? So, don't break the promise you make to yourself either.

Are you overwhelmed or not ready for a list? Then take one tiny step at a time towards your desired future. Each day, ask yourself, "What can I do today that will improve my life?" Just one thing. Then, do it! The next day, add two things. Once that positive momentum begins, there's no turning back.

Monitoring Areas of Success

Who decides if you are successful? You do! Society often leads you to believe that success is measured by wealth, luxurious homes, flashy cars, and expensive jewelry. However, success can take many forms, and it varies from person to person. In different aspects of your life, there are many ways to achieve success, and it's completely normal to excel in some areas while facing challenges in others.

Being perfect in everything all the time is not likely. Perfection doesn't exist. Success is personal, so comparing yourself to others makes little sense because everyone is so vastly different. You are your own measure; you are your own competition in your own unique ways of being successful. So, focus on these areas:

1. **Financial Success:** Focuses on your money situation. While money isn't the most important thing, you need it to live and enjoy things like vacations or material things, if that's what you like.
2. **Career Success:** This is about your job. Do you enjoy what you do, or is it time to try something new? Having the right career can have a big impact.
3. **Influence Success:** Making a positive difference in the world. You can help people, protect the environment, or take care of animals. If this is important to you, it's a great area to focus on.

4. **Family and Relationship Success:** How you are with your family and friends? Some people are naturally good at being a parent or partner, while others might want to give more attention and energy here.
5. **Health Success:** How do you take care of yourself? Are you eating healthy and exercising regularly?
6. **Soul Success:** What makes you happy and keeps you excited about life? What activities do you love doing?
7. **Internal Success:** Where is your mindset? How much do you love and respect yourself and what's your overall attitude towards life?

This isn't about pointing out your failures. It's about looking at where you do well and where you might need to improve to grow. What success means to you is special because it depends on what you find important. Someone might have lots of money but feel empty without family. Think about what you value and find your strengths and areas you need to work on to have a more balanced and happy life.

Remember

Be your own hero and love yourself as much as you want to be loved. Understand your purpose and worth. Believe in yourself. You belong here or else you wouldn't be here. You are here for a reason; nothing is by accident. You have an amazing life to live.

Find your path to success and act for change. Remember, what you focus on grows. Think about the good things you want and work towards them. When you feel sad or angry, recognize your feelings; don't hide or ignore them. Work through these emotions and let go of what doesn't serve you.

Connect with yourself. Listen to your inner voice and take care of your soul, seeing life as something happening *for* you. Understand that life's journey includes ups and downs and see challenges as chances to grow.

Perfection does not exist; it's normal to make mistakes and have tough days. You will meet people who are hurting and might take it out on you. Handle these moments with kindness to yourself and view them with compassion in your heart.

Your time and energy are valuable, so spend them wisely with people who love, cherish, and respect you. It's okay to say no. Think about what your future self would advise. Look at your current thoughts and consider what steps you can take to improve your life today. Set your goals and commit to changes. Keep your promises to yourself.

One of my favorite quotes from Gandhi is, "Be the change you wish to see in the world." So, be the change you want to see in yourself. Only you decide your value and direction. It's your choice. Forgive yourself and others.

One day at a time. That's all it takes. I believe in you!

About Brandy Lovingier

Brandy Lovingier is a dedicated Board-Certified Hypnotherapist, NLP, EFT, and TIME Techniques Practitioner, as well as a Success Life Coach with over seven years of experience. She specializes in empowering women, children, and animals to navigate life's challenges by releasing stuck emotions and overcoming negative thoughts or experiences.

Through her holistic approach, Brandy helps clients overcome loss, set actionable goals, and release stagnant energy to achieve inner peace. Her compassionate work extends to animals in distress, providing support for animals suffering from past abuse or during times of transition, while offering comfort to their owners.

As a Double Certified Reiki Master Trainer, Brandy brings a deep understanding of energy healing for both humans and animals. Her commitment to clients fosters emotional resilience for a more positive outlook, to reclaim their lives and find balance. Through her work, she inspires, transforms, and supports individuals on their journey towards overall wellness and fulfillment.

To get Brandy's gift:

www.InnerRevolutionBook.com/gift/Brandy

Your time and energy are valuable, so spend them wisely with people who love, cherish, and respect you.

Inner Revolution: Embracing Change to Achieve Greatness

Become A Proactive Business Owner

Fernanda Diaz, MNLP, MTT, MHt, MSC, and Trainer of NLP

After 12 years as a Life and Business Coach and seven years in Human Resources across various industries, I've noticed a striking pattern: employee engagement and satisfaction aren't driven by salary or financial perks, but by genuine care for employees and a stable work environment.

The COVID-19 pandemic has fundamentally shifted the workplace landscape, rendering outdated paradigms and mindsets obsolete. This transformation presents a crucial opportunity for businesses to reevaluate their strategies. Are you wasting time, resources, and money reacting to issues rather than proactively addressing them?

Redefining Your Business's Trajectory

In this chapter, we will explore the key topics that can redefine your business's trajectory, setting you on a path toward greater employee retention and overall success.

Solving Issues vs BEing PROACTIVE

A) Solving Issues: Over 90% of the time when I ask about the vision, mission, and values of the company, leaders, directors, or team members are not clear or don't even know them.

The vision, mission, and values of the company haven't been updated to the present times or are not being taken into consideration when decision-making.

Directors are doing their best with their knowledge to grow the company. As a result, every director has their vision and values, and everyone is pulling in their direction.

Often, I see business owner's complete burnout from putting out fires. When I asked them about the vision of why this company was created, they could not even remember, because it was created as part of the to-do list to be the shiny object for the webpage or employee manual.

A) PROACTIVE: Your vision, mission, and values as a business owner define who you are and serve as the motivation behind your daily commitment to invest time, energy, effort, and money in your company.

By being clear on your vision, mission, and values, you will hire like-minded people who share the same values and are excited to be part of your vision.

By fostering loyal relationships with your employees, you can reduce turnover rates, which can be costly for companies.

Putting your vision, mission, and values in the first place when decision-making or creating procedures will sort out the ones that do not align with the vision of the company, avoiding future regrets and saving time and money.

B) Solving Issues: Training your team 100% in Hard Skills: Did you know that ONLY 20% of success is determined by the knowledge gained through education? Your company only focuses its training on technical material or software.

Training only a portion of your team in soft skills—specifically owners, head directors, and team leaders—is crucial, as their technical knowledge alone is insufficient for effectively managing personnel.

B) PROACTIVE: Training your people in hard skills and soft skills will allow you to tap into the other 80% to achieve Success.

Essential training courses include effective communication, leadership, time, and project management, teamwork, flexibility, and adaptability to new markets.

When the company, including directors, leaders, and team members, is part of the same training, it creates a special connection, and a sense of camaraderie and belonging, which will allow flexibility in projects.

Team members are more willing to adapt to recent changes.

New projects are easily and effortlessly taken into action when the entire team takes part in creating them, instead of being imposed.

C) Solving Issues: Creation of procedures and taking decisions are only being made by owners and head directors who are no longer involved in the day-to-day operations.

Having a global view of the company and strategies to expand is the responsibility of owners and head directors, but if these decisions are made without an internal point of view, it will lead to delays and obstacles in projects that could have been avoided easily.

C) PROACTIVE: To be effective when decision making it's important to have at least two team members 100% involved in operations and have no power position.

These team members will tell you what is possible or not based on the current operations or will identify obstacles in the way.

D) Solving Issues: Decisions are being made by leaders, owners, and head directors who have been working for the company for 10+ years; YES, these team leaders know the company and while they were focused on it, the world changed and new social approaches, new technologies, and new marketing strategies have taken over the market.

D) PROACTIVE: Open your decision-making meetings to recent graduates. They don't know your company the way you do, plus THEY ARE the new market.

E) Solving Issues: 100% of the resources of the company are put into product development, marketing, and sales strategies.

Zero percent to minimum resources are dedicated to personal growth or career building for employees.

E) PROACTIVE: As business owners, we need to understand that the success or failure of our company is based on the quality of the people who collaborate with us. Their well-being is our company's well-being. As leaders, we need to build relationships and care for their growth if we want them to care for our company's growth.

F) Solving Issues: All activities are professionally related to incentive sales or marketing.

F) PROACTIVE: Create an environment where your employees feel valued for who they are, not just for what they do. Create family days, potluck days, wellness days—any activity non-work related where you can see the person behind the title.

G) Solving Issues: Outdated or nonexistent:

- Day-to-day duties and responsibilities,
- Goals and expectations for the year,
- Employee Manual Procedures.

When business owners tell me about an issue with a specific position, they blame the employee. I ask to see the mentioned list and 80% of the time it's nonexistent or completely outdated.

Then how do we expect any employee to be held accountable if there is nothing in writing that will lead the person on how to perform or manage any situation?

If the documents exist, they are not used as a guide for performance.

G) PROACTIVE: The Employee Manual is a living manual, changing and adapting to the new endeavors of the company.

Every Roll in the company has their day-to-day duties and responsibilities. These are used as guidance to train new employees and are updated every time there is a new system in place. The employee in the role is the one in charge of keeping this document updated.

Every employee has their own goals and expectations for the new year. These are set in the last month of the year or the first two weeks of the new year and are broken into trimester achievements with real, measurable, and tangible expectations. Supervisors consider these projections to direct the actions of their staff.

H) Solving Issues: Managers are running the company.

Employees can work for the managers and will cover their to-do list, but they won't go the extra mile if needed; the success rate is 50% or less.

H) PROACTIVE: The company is being run by leaders who are managers.

Leaders create relationships, employees love to work for leaders, and the success rate is 70% or higher.

The Cost of Improvement

The first question I get when exposed to the presumable lack is: What will this cost to fix and how long will it take?

Business Owners will try to make everything: FAST, GOOD, and CHEAP. These variables have the following characteristics:

- If you need it, FAST and GOOD: It's going to be expensive.

- When you want it, CHEAP and GOOD: It's going to take a long time.
- If you want it, FAST and CHEAP: It will not be good... and I won't take you as a client because of my vision and values.

But there is a different approach you can take, especially for someone who is starting or who loves to be involved 360 degrees in their company.

Become a Proactive Business Owner

To transition from reactive to proactive, follow these five steps:

1. Values:

Your company's stated values form its core structure. They guide decision-making and shape the culture of your organization. Many business owners overlook how crucial and unique their values are, yet they play a vital role in defining the personnel you hire and how they represent your company.

Your company's values should align with your own core beliefs, so focus on identifying your top three personal values. The order of these values matters just as much as the values themselves. They reflect how you prioritize your time, decide, and perceive the world.

When you hire individuals who share these core values, you create a sense of understanding and alignment. This shared foundation makes it easier to collaborate and innovate together.

2. Vision and Mission:

Why do you wake up each day and give 100% to your business? What motivates you during challenging times? The answers to these questions should be deeply rooted in your passion, as this enthusiasm is the heart of your business.

When I was 23, I launched my first business—a real estate company in Argentina. I made it a priority to ensure that both my employees and clients knew the purpose behind my business and who our primary clients were. I discovered that when I shared my truth, including the challenges I aimed to address and the positive impacts I hoped to create, many more people were willing to help.

Clients transitioned from being mere transactions to becoming integral parts of my mission and vision. This created a sense of belonging to something greater than simply renting an apartment, prompting them to happily share my business with their friends.

This shift in perspective allowed me to move from spending on high-cost advertising and cold calling to enjoying a referral-based business model, where clients naturally brought in more clients.

My company's core values were accountability, transparency, and stability.

Vision: To be the leading real estate business in Buenos Aires, focusing on easing the process for immigrant college students seeking long-term rentals.

Mission: To provide a worry-free experience for tenants and landlords by managing all legal, liability, and insurance processes—no guarantor needed.

By communicating to landlords that my clients were immigrant college students, they recognized their role in fostering a welcoming environment and contributing to the student's sense of stability and belonging. Having once been that immigrant student who struggled to find housing without financial backing, I understood their needs firsthand. This empathy resonated not only with landlords but also with the students themselves. As they shared their positive experiences, I found myself with a consistent stream of tenants, effectively eliminating the struggle for listings.

3. **Day-to-Day Duties and Responsibilities:**

Clearly defining day-to-day duties for every role helps new hires align with the company's vision. It clarifies expectations and highlights when performance is lacking, leaving no room for misunderstandings, and fostering transparency.

Begin with your role, ensuring everyone—employees and clients alike—understands your contributions and what's expected of them. When everyone knows their roles, it encourages open communication, reduces confusion in task assignments, and leads to timely project completion.

4. Yearly Goals and Expectations:

Many companies set annual goals just to check a box. However, when done effectively, these goals can guide your weekly actions and decisions, preventing you from feeling lost among multiple employees. With a glance, you can see what everyone is focusing on, track weekly objectives, and assess progress toward annual goals.

Begin by establishing your own goals that align with your mission, vision, and values. Communicate these goals clearly to hold yourself accountable, ensuring everyone is on the same page.

5. Employee Manual Procedures:

Each new employee will receive an introductory guide along with an official document outlining procedures. This approach minimizes surprises and prevents the need to reinvent the wheel. If a challenging situation arises without an existing procedure, it signals that you need to create one.

Embrace Proactivity

The change of your company starts with you; BECOMING that proactive entrepreneur, serving as an example for your people, and holding you and them accountable are important steps towards a successful business. When you are there, and you like what you have created, say this aloud:

"And I learned to stay here because it's the most beautiful scene I have ever created."

Inner Revolution: Embracing Change to Achieve Greatness

About Fernanda Diaz

Fernanda Diaz is an International Speaker, Life & Business Coach and Meditation Instructor with 12 years of experience empowering managers, leaders, entrepreneurs, and their teams to become their best selves. She facilitates core transformations that create a profound impact on their lives, businesses, and communities.

Originally from Ecuador, Fernanda expanded her coaching journey to Mexico and Argentina, where she lived for eight years and met her husband. They have two sons and have resided in the United States for the past seven years.

Fernanda holds numerous certifications, including the Professional Ontological Coach, Mindfulness & Meditation Coach, Clinical Hypnotherapist Trainer, EFT Trainer, TIME Techniques Trainer, Neuro-Linguistic Programming Trainer and Life & Success Coach Trainer.

Her primary passion lies in conducting in-person workshops, where she employs science-based methods to elevate participants' awareness and consciousness, opening doors to new possibilities. Her favorite workshops focus on team building and leadership, helping individuals unlock their potential and foster collaboration.

Get Fernanda's gift:

www.InnerRevolutionBook.com/gift/Fernanda

Inner Revolution: Embracing Change to Achieve Greatness

Change Is an Inside Job

Joanne Klepal, NLPMP, MTT, MHt, MSC, CCHt, RMT, CCMP™

"Change is never painful. Only resistance to change is painful." — Buddha

You often hear that "change is hard," that you are "saturated with change," suffer from "change fatigue," or you tell yourself, "I don't like change." This belief that change is difficult is deeply embedded in your psyche, affecting your mindset, draining your mental, physical, and emotional energy.

Yet, without change, you would still dwell in caves, gathering food, manually washing clothes, traveling by horse-drawn carriages, and visiting libraries for research. You certainly wouldn't enjoy the luxuries of instant communication, global travel in mere hours instead of weeks, and managing your life through a compact, handheld device.

And yet why is it when you start a change you truly desire, be it a new job, a relationship, or an upgraded phone, you feel excitement and even experience butterflies?

Change is the Law of the Universe

You are increasingly living in a state of constant change. Change is no longer an exception; it has become the rule, the standard. Remaining static is like never updating your phone or computer operating system. I'm here to let you in on a secret. Change doesn't have to be hard. Let's first explore why change might seem challenging.

What You Didn't Know About Change

Your Conscious & Subconscious Must Align

Going on vacation with your partner is much smoother when you both agree and are aligned with the destination, isn't it? This is the same with your mind.

Consider your mind as an iceberg. There is a small portion visible above the surface, and a significantly larger portion hidden beneath it.

Which part of the iceberg do you believe takes up more space and drives the most movement? Correct. It's the unseen portion below the surface.

Similarly, your mind comprises the conscious part, of which you are aware, and the subconscious part, of which you are not. It is the subconscious that is larger and drives significant change.

Now consider your online banking application. As a user, you are limited to using the app for what it was programmed to do. For instance, if you wish to view transactions from 20 years ago but the app is designed to only display up to ten, you will encounter an error. The only way to align this is to reprogram and update the software.

Similarly, to effect enduring and positive change, you must reprogram your subconscious mind to be in harmony with your conscious mind. They must operate in unison. As Micheal Stevenson says: "Trying to live your entire life with

Inner Revolution: Embracing Change to Achieve Greatness

your unconscious [1] mind is like trying to win a poker tournament with only one card."

You might be curious about how your subconscious is programmed. It starts from birth, and there are three key periods [2] where your beliefs and value systems take shape: the imprint period (0-7 years), modeling period (8-13 years), and socialization period (14-21 years).

The imprint period is crucial because the mind, like a sponge, absorbs everything without filters, and critical thinking hasn't developed yet. Brainwave states are in alpha and theta, akin to a meditative or trance-like state, making you highly suggestible with a vivid imagination. It's during this time that the subconscious is intensely programmed, forming many of your fundamental beliefs and values, particularly from influential figures like parents and teachers.

The adage "give me the child until seven and I'll show you the man" underscores the significance of subconscious programming at a young age.

During the modeling period, critical and analytical thinking develops, and influences expand to include public figures and superheroes.

The socialization period sees a significant influence from peers, and there may be a push back against earlier programming. Those with teenagers will relate to this phase.

So, if you're struggling with change and achieving what you desire, for instance, if you're consciously aiming for a financial goal but face continuous challenges, it might be time to examine your subconscious programming, specifically your ingrained beliefs and values. Holding on to beliefs such as "it takes money to make money," "nothing comes easy," or "money is the root of all evil" shows a misalignment between your conscious goals and subconscious programming.

There are Multiple Layers of Change

Change, like the layers of an onion, has various levels, each with its own significance and impact on the conscious and subconscious mind. Let's explore these layers with an example.

Imagine you aim to improve your health and slim down by twelve pounds. You might join a gym or buy an exercise bike, starting with great enthusiasm. However, this excitement and initial burst of motivation often quickly wanes because it's a change to your external **environment**.

You might also try changing your **behavior** by eating healthier, like opting for salads at lunch. But how long before this becomes boring and burdensome?

Altering just your external environment and/or behavior requires immense effort and discipline, which is often unsustainable. The subsequent layers [3] are where true transformation happens by addressing your program and motivational factors.

Beliefs are convictions you hold as true. They function like a switch, either empowering or disempowering you; there's no middle ground.

Values define what's important to you, guiding your judgments of actions as good or bad, right or wrong. They drive your actions and determine your willingness to act or refrain.

Identity is your self-conception, who you believe you are, and is built on your values and beliefs. It often starts with the most powerful words, "I am..."

Consider how challenging it would be to lose weight if you harbor beliefs like "losing weight is too hard" or "I must clean my plate" or if you value "not wasting food." What if your identity is tied to being obese or unworthy?

Without addressing these deeper layers, altering your environment or behavior alone will always be a struggle. But by changing your disempowering beliefs and aligning your values and identity, you can truly achieve a healthier, slimmer body.

Change Is an Inside Job

In today's world, you are inundated with messages from various channels insisting that you need certain products to be "complete" or to be "fixed." Change is an inside job and requires active participation from you. The more profound the internal exploration into aspects such as beliefs, values, and identity, the more significant the change and the greater your success.

I frequently hear things like: "I'll be happy when I..." or "I want to feel confident, passion, peace, etc." These statements are just internal states of being. You need nothing external to feel these states, and you can change your state instantly with tools such as anchors or tapping.

You Don't Fear Change

Recall a moment in your life when a change seemed frightening, yet in retrospect, it turned out to be the best event that ever occurred.

The fear wasn't in the change itself, but in the transition to the unknown—the interim between the familiar and the undiscovered. So, take a lesson from the butterfly; get comfortable and embrace the unknown.

You're Here to Improve

What drives your desire for change? Is it for your own benefit or for someone else's? Change that is motivated by others' desires is often short-lived. Remember, you're not here to "prove," you're here to improve.

Tools to Make Change Easy

Now that you know why change can appear to be hard, let's look at some tools to help you achieve your greatness.

Self-Hypnosis

Self-hypnosis is a powerful tool for changing and improving thoughts, beliefs, behaviors, and emotions. Like meditation, it increases self-awareness and uses the power of suggestion to help you achieve success.

Self-hypnosis is not about losing control or something that "happens" to you as misrepresented in movies or comedy shows. It's an intentional, self-induced, trance-like state.

For instance, when you're completely absorbed in an activity such as gardening or reading, and time seems to slip away, or when you drive home on autopilot without remembering the trip, you're experiencing a trance-like state.

Self-hypnosis enables you to access alpha and theta brainwave states, opening a door to harmonize, align, and positively influence your conscious and subconscious minds.

Here are eight simple steps to self-hypnotize:

1. Find a quiet, comfortable, and undisturbed place to relax.

2. Bring awareness to each part of your body, from toes to head, tensing and then allowing complete relaxation.

3. Set a clear and positive intention or goal, such as increasing confidence, improving memory, or enhancing sleep. Ask yourself: "How will my life improve when I achieve this?" "What will I be doing once I've succeeded?" "Where, when, and how will I do it?" and "Who will be with me?"

4. Enter a meditative state by relaxing your body and mind. Breathe slowly and deeply. Let your eyes rest, and with each exhale, feel your eyes grow heavier until they're too heavy to open. (Use relaxing background music if it helps).

5. Continue to relax deeply, visualizing yourself descending a staircase of ten steps. With each step down, relax further and feel your body grow heavier.

6. In this deeply relaxed state, focus on your intention or goal, using the information you've outlined.

7. Affirm your goal with direct, positive statements. Keep it concise, such as "I am..." Repeat each affirmation at least three times.

8. Gradually return to full awareness by imagining yourself ascending the stairs, becoming more alert with each step. At the top step, gently open your eyes, fully returning to your surroundings.

Enjoy and let yourself be filled with amazement and gratitude for the incredible achievements you accomplish through self-hypnosis!

Layers of Change and Beliefs

Once you have defined the specific outcome you want, go through the layers of change, and ask yourself:

- Identity: Who do I have to become?
- Values: What needs to become important to me?
- Beliefs: What must I believe?

- Resources/Potential: What resources or skills do I have or need?
- Behaviors: What behaviors do I need to develop, change, or stop? What must I do that I do not want to?
- Environment: What do I need to change in my environment?
- Who can I model and what do they do? (e.g., Richard Branson, Tony Robbins)

If you need to dig deeper into your beliefs, particularly ones that may be holding you back, ask yourself:

- What is my belief?
- Why do I believe it?
- What am I afraid would happen if I didn't believe that?
- What is the belief protecting me from, and do I really believe that?
- Whose belief is it, anyway?
- What can I choose to believe instead? What belief will empower and support me?

There are a multitude of tools available to help delve deeper into yourself. Here are some more of my favorites:

Reiki, a deeply relaxing energy technique, soothes the mind and body, allowing brainwaves to transition into alpha and theta states, enhancing focus and clarity.

Yoga, which encompasses breathwork, mantra chanting, and meditation, is often celebrated for its physical advantages. Yet, recent scientific studies have also highlighted its beneficial impacts on brain function and hormonal and glandular changes.

Both Reiki and yoga are excellent for accessing the subconscious and addressing changes on physical, mental, emotional, and energetic levels. During the restful states of Reiki and yoga, I often engage in self-hypnosis.

Emotional Freedom Techniques (EFT), known as tapping, along with anchoring, can swiftly alter one's internal state.

Neuro-Linguistic Programming (NLP) techniques, including anchoring, sub-modality shifts, TIME™ Techniques, and Personal Breakthrough Experiences, are superb for quickly altering mindsets and updating old beliefs, values, and identities, and aligning the conscious and subconscious minds.

"To embrace life is to embrace change, to embrace change is to achieve greatness." — Joanne Klepal

Now that you know **change can be easy**, befriend your subconscious and uncertainty, and welcome the unknown. Embrace change and achieve your greatness!

---

[1] Unconscious and subconscious are used interchangeably.

[2] Morris Massey.

[3] *There is a layer between behavior and beliefs known as resources or potential, which I have not covered here.*

About Joanne Klepal

Joanne Klepal, founder of Live Your Yellow Brick Road and YogaMeetsU.com, is an expert in change and transformation, and is deeply passionate about ongoing personal growth and development. Her purpose is to elevate the frequency of humanity and help women become unstuck, empowering them to consciously create and live their life filled with purpose.

Known for her calm presence, Joanne brings a unique approach to personal transformation, leveraging both the science and art of change. She holds certifications as a Master Practitioner of Neuro-Linguistic Programming (NLP) & NLP Coaching, Master Practitioner of TIME Techniques, Clinical Hypnotherapist, Change Management Professional™, and Reiki Master Trainer.

Additionally, Joanne is a Kundalini Yoga Instructor, breathwork practitioner, and the best-selling author of *Mastery of the Mind: The Pathway to Empowerment,* and *Natural Healing Techniques: Get Well & Stay Well with Asian Bio-Energetic Therapy.*

Go to www.liveyouryellowbrickroad.com to discover more.

For your free gift from Joanne:

www.InnerRevolutionBook.com/gift/Joanne

Inner Revolution: Embracing Change to Achieve Greatness

Change Your Language: Change Your Results!

Sam Wakefield, Sales Expert

Language matters. In sales, in leadership, in personal relationships—words hold power. The right words can open doors, shift perspectives, and build connections, while the wrong ones can create distance, misunderstanding, and even resistance. In my journey through sales and coaching, I've seen firsthand how simple language adjustments can lead to monumental changes in results. Language isn't just a tool for communication; it's a tool for transformation.

The words we choose frame not only how others perceive us but also how we perceive ourselves. They shape our mindset, influence our actions, and ultimately define our outcomes. By becoming intentional with language, you're not only enhancing your ability to connect with clients but also transforming your self-image and expanding your potential. In this chapter, we'll explore the art of using language as a catalyst for change. You'll discover strategies to improve your interactions, increase your influence, and achieve the results you've always envisioned.

The Subtle Power of Word Choice: "Interested" vs. "Open"

Let's start with a simple, yet powerful example of language transformation: using the word "open" instead of "interested." When we ask someone if they're "interested" in an idea or opportunity, there's an assumption that they're already knowledgeable about the topic or have formed some level of curiosity. But here's the truth—no one can be genuinely interested in something they don't fully understand or are unfamiliar with.

The word open, however, invites curiosity without any pretense of understanding. "Are you open to exploring this idea?" feels less intrusive and more inviting. The word "open" appeals to people's desire to be perceived as open-minded rather than closed off. In sales, this subtle shift lowers resistance and creates a more receptive atmosphere. When you ask someone if they're open, you're not forcing them to take a stance; you're simply inviting them to explore possibilities. This difference, while subtle, leads to drastically improved outcomes in conversations and negotiations.

Imagine this scenario: you're meeting a potential client for the first time, and you ask, "Would you be interested in our product?" There's an implied expectation in that question, one that may make the client feel pressured. Now, consider rephrasing it as, "Would you be open to hearing how our product could benefit you?" Suddenly, the conversation feels more collaborative, less pushy, and more focused on the client's potential gain. This simple adjustment can be the difference between a polite "I'll think about it" and a genuine engagement that leads to a successful close.

Rapport-Building Language: The Power of "We"

Rapport is essential in any successful sales interaction. It's the foundation that allows trust to flourish, making clients feel comfortable enough to open up about their needs and concerns. At Close It Now, one of our core principles is that effective sales are rooted in connection, not coercion. We teach that rapport is built not just by what we say but by how we say it, and the words we choose can either strengthen or weaken that connection.

One of the easiest ways to build rapport is through the use of inclusive language, particularly the word we. When you use "we," you're creating a sense of partnership, of shared goals. Instead of saying, "I think this solution will work for you," say, "Together, we can find a solution that fits your needs." This shift in language aligns you with the client's journey, making you a collaborator in their success rather than an outsider selling a product.

Consider a scenario where you're presenting options to a client. You might say, "We're in this together, and I'm here to help you find the best choice." This approach positions you as an ally rather than an adversary, someone who is genuinely invested in the client's success. Language like this dissolves barriers, inviting the client to view you as a trusted advisor rather than a salesperson.

Transformative Phrasing: Focusing on Potential, Not Problems

In sales, the way we frame solutions can drastically affect the client's perception. At Close It Now, we emphasize transformative phrasing—using language that emphasizes potential and positive outcomes rather than just addressing problems. This approach taps into the emotional side of decision-making, helping clients envision the benefits rather than focusing solely on fixing issues.

For instance, rather than saying, "This will prevent your system from breaking down," try saying, "This will ensure your system operates at peak performance, providing you with comfort and peace of mind." The first statement is reactive, addressing a potential issue. The second statement is proactive, focusing on a vision of a positive future. By framing the conversation around possibilities, you create an emotional connection to the solution, one that resonates on a deeper level.

Another example could be in offering a product upgrade. Instead of saying, "This upgrade will solve your current problems," try, "This upgrade will enhance your experience, providing added comfort and reliability for years to come." Notice how this phrasing doesn't just address a problem—it elevates the conversation to one of improvement, growth, and long-term satisfaction.

Reframing Self-Talk: Language Shapes Self-Perception

Language isn't only powerful in external conversations; it profoundly affects our internal dialogue as well. At Close It Now, we believe that the words we use to describe ourselves and our abilities can either empower us or limit us. Self-talk—those internal conversations we have daily—shapes our beliefs, attitudes, and ultimately, our results.

Consider the difference between saying, "I'll try to close this deal" versus "I will close this deal by aligning with what the client truly needs." The word try introduces doubt and lack of commitment. On the other hand, the phrase I will implies certainty, determination, and a clear vision of success. By choosing words that affirm our abilities, we strengthen our resolve and increase our chances of achieving our goals.

Another example is replacing "I have to" with "I get to." When you say, "I have to make this sales call," it implies obligation and burden. However, "I get to make this sales call" shifts the perspective to one of privilege and opportunity. This slight reframe has a powerful effect on mindset, transforming mundane tasks into purposeful actions that contribute to personal and professional growth.

Making Clients Feel Valued Through Language

One of the best ways to stand out in sales is to make clients feel truly valued. This doesn't happen through generic phrases or scripted lines—it requires personalization and genuine acknowledgment. In Close It Now training, we teach sales professionals how to use language to create memorable moments, making clients feel seen and appreciated.

For instance, instead of saying, "Thank you for your time," add a specific observation that shows you were paying attention. Say, "Thank you for sharing your vision for your home with me. It's clear that you're passionate about creating a comfortable environment for your family." This level of personalization makes the client feel special and strengthens the connection, enhancing trust and loyalty.

Anchoring Positive Emotions: The Power of Visualization

Another technique we use in Close It Now is anchoring positive emotions through language. This is particularly effective during closing moments. Clients often make decisions based on how they feel in the moment, even if they rationalize their choices later. By anchoring positive emotions to the language we use, we create an experience that resonates beyond the immediate transaction.

For example, when discussing a long-term solution, you might say, "Imagine the peace of mind you'll feel knowing this investment will benefit you for years to come." This phrase doesn't just describe the product; it invites the client to visualize the emotional outcome—peace of mind, security, and satisfaction. These emotions become anchored to their decision, reinforcing the positive feelings associated with the choice.

Repetition and Reinforcement: Solidifying Key Messages

In high-stakes sales, it's crucial to reinforce key messages subtly throughout the conversation. People often need to hear an idea multiple times before it fully resonates. One technique we teach at Close It Now is the art of strategic repetition—repeating essential points using varied phrasing, so clients internalize the message without feeling pressured.

For instance, if you're discussing an energy-efficient upgrade, you might start by saying, "This option is energy-efficient, saving you money over time." Later in the conversation, reinforce it with, "Think of the long-term savings and reduced environmental impact this choice offers." By restating the benefits in different ways, you solidify the concept in the client's mind, making the value of the investment clear.

Language as a Tool for Ethical Influence

It's important to remember that language is a tool for ethical influence, not manipulation. At Close It Now, we emphasize the importance of integrity in every interaction. Authenticity is at the heart of our approach. When you're transparent and genuine, clients can feel it—they know when you're truly invested in their best interests.

Using language ethically means focusing on the client's needs rather than pushing your own agenda. It's about guiding them to a solution that genuinely benefits them, even if it means not closing a deal immediately. Ethical language builds trust, and in the long run, this trust leads to referrals, repeat business, and a reputation as someone who truly cares.

Conclusion: Harness the Power of Language to Transform Your Results

Language isn't just about communication; it's about transformation. By becoming intentional with your words, you're opening doors, creating connections, and building a path toward success. Each conversation becomes an opportunity not just to sell, but to inspire, uplift, and empower.

Remember, every word you choose creates an impact. The small shifts—asking if someone is open rather than interested, using we instead of I, framing solutions as opportunities—are the keys to unlocking greater results. In sales and in life, language is your greatest tool. Use it wisely, and watch as it changes not only your interactions but your entire approach to success.

About Sam Wakefield

Sam Wakefield is a leading expert in sales training for the HVAC and home services industries, boasting 20 years of experience in transforming sales teams and individuals into top performers. As the founder and host of the Close It Now Sales Training podcast, Sam delivers actionable insights and innovative strategies that seamlessly blend psychology, empathy, and proven systems, empowering sales professionals to achieve remarkable success.

Driven by a deep passion for teaching, Sam believes that ethical sales practices foster long-term relationships and sustainable business growth. He is an award-winning coach, keynote speaker, and author dedicated to unlocking the potential of others, equipping them to close more deals with confidence and integrity.

Sam's mission is clear and compelling: to empower professionals to sell smarter, serve better, and succeed faster. Through his expertise and unwavering commitment, he inspires a new generation of sales leaders to reach their fullest potential.

Get a free gift from Sam by visiting:

www.InnerRevolutionBook.com/gift/Sam

Made in the USA
Monee, IL
08 December 2024

72932332R00144